W

GOD'S CHILDREN

We Are All God's Children

Joseph Haddad

DERUSHA PUBLISHING LLC • FT. LEE

ISBN: 978-1-935104-01-8

ISBN-10: 1-935104-01-2

Books published by Derusha Publishing LLC may be purchased for educational, business, or sales promotional use. For more information, please write:

Special Markets Department
Derusha Publishing LLC
407 Jane St (2nd Floor)
Fort Lee, NJ 07024
USA

Derusha Publishing is committed to preserving ancient forests and natural resources. We elected to print this title on 100% postconsumer recycled paper, processed chlorine-free. As a result, we have saved:

7 Trees (40' tall and 6-8" diameter)
2 Million BTUs of Total Energy
641 Pounds of Greenhouse Gases
3,086 Gallons of Wastewater
187 Pounds of Solid Waste

Derusha Publishing made this paper choice because our printer, Thomson-Shore, Inc., is a member of Green Press Initiative, a nonprofit program dedicated to supporting authors, publishers, and suppliers in their efforts to reduce their use of fiber obtained from endangered forests.

For more information, visit www.greenpressinitiative.org

Environmental impact estimates were made using the Environmental Defense Paper Calculator. For more information visit: www.edf.org/papercalculator

To My Children

Rachel, Freda, Rebecca, Deborah, Samuel, Sarah, Lauren

Through Them I See All God's Children

Acknowledgments

Authoring this work has been a labor of love. For a professional businessperson, making time for creative writing and sustained thought is not a simple task.

"Make for yourself a *Rav*" is the directive in *Ethics of the Fathers*. Jewish tradition teaches that each of us must appoint a Rabbi – a spiritual mentor – to help guide us in our personal development.

I would like to acknowledge and express my thanks and gratitude to the spiritual mentors I have had the privilege of making for myself in my adult years.

Rabbi Ezra Labaton, Rabbi of Congregation Magen David of West Deal NJ, has taught me to appreciate scholarship and value open inquiry and truth – no matter where it lies. The years and time we spent learning privately are among my fondest and most rewarding. His cherubic demeanor belies his warmth, depth and commitment.

Rabbi Dr. Shlomo Riskin, Chief Rabbi of the city of Efrat, Israel, provides me with an inspiring and ongoing role model of erudition, leadership, accomplishment and dedication to Jewish and the finest of universal values.

Rabbi Professor José Faur, of Bar Ilan University, is simply one of the finest minds of our day – a true "*Gadol Hador*." His works will be studied for generations to come, who will benefit from his vast erudition and penetrating intellect. He is a Rabbi's Rabbi and a professors professor. Yet he is accessible and so passionate in embracing the notion of the perfectibility of man.

In a generation so sorely lacking in true and effective leadership, these individuals positively influenced my development (and that of so many others). The positive ideas in this volume are a reflection of their teachings.

JOSEPH HADDAD
July 15, 2009
Ranana, Israel

Foreword

HEBREW HUMANISM is grounded on the belief that we all are the children of Adam and Eve, and that they were endowed with the "image of God," which God implanted within them. The "image of God" is the patrimony of every one of Adam's and Eve's descendents, including Noah's children and their posterity (see *Gn* 9:6). Thus, the HEBREW SCRIPTURE is the ESSENCE OF RELIGIOUS HUMANISM, since He created every human being in "His image." In this pivotal point, the God of the Hebrew Scripture differs radically from the God of either the Christian or Moslem Scripture. In quality of *Father*, the God of Israel speaks *directly* to His *children*, from Adam to Malachi, the last Prophet of Israel. Although the Christian Scripture ascertains that Jesus spoke to God, it never says that God spoke to Jesus. Likewise, in the Moslem Scripture the angel Gabriel is said to speak to Mohammed, never God Himself! Again, the God of the Hebrew Scripture came down and spoke directly to His children at Sinai. In Christian and Moslem tradition, Jesus and Mohammed *ascend* to heaven (*post mortem*); God, however, never *descends* to speak to them on earth, in the presence of the entire community. In Israel, God is not only the Father of the people, but also their *King* – that is, He is the *Sovereign* of the people. Accordingly, He issues a series of directives (the 613 *miṣvot*) to be *implemented* down here on earth, affecting the daily life of the *individual*, the *family*, the *community*, and the *nation*. This is why Rabbinic tradition refers to Moses as God's Emissary [Hebrew: *Shaliaḥ*; Arabic: *Rasul*]. Therefore, in reference to Moses – and Moses alone – the Hebrew Scripture says, "And God spoke to Moses, saying: Speak to the children of Israel, and say to them…." Nothing of this sort is to be found in the Christian and Moslem Scriptures, respectively, in reference to either Jesus or Mohammed. Finally, since the God of Israel is the God of all humanity, every human being – and not only Jews – can gain salvation. Hence, the Rabbinic doctrine: *ḥaside ummot ha-ʻolam yesh lahem ḥeleq le-ʻolam ha-ba*, "the pious among the nations have a portion in the world to come" – in other words, they shall be saved. This was pointed out by Maimonides, with one *caveat*: they must fulfill the seven Noahide precepts, because of Moses's authority that revealed that Noah's children had accepted, early in history, these precepts (see *MT Melakhim* 8:11). The rationale is simple: only Moses, by having been consecrated as God's Emissary by God Himself at Sinai, has the mandate to transmit precepts in His name. Put differently, in the Hebrew mind, 'salvation' is predicated on accepting God's *Dominion* (Hebrew: *malkhut*), '*sovereignty*' on earth. His Dominion is effected by implementing the *miṣvot* which He delivered through Moses. These are 613 *miṣvot* if you are a member of the Congregation of Israel, having contracted a Covenant with God at Sinai – 7 *miṣvot* if you are a member of "the family of nations" stemming from Noah's children (*Gn* 10:32).

Joseph Haddad, the author of this book, is a man that walks the paths of the Tora and has grasped the subtleties involved in this special form of religious humanism, embracing the children of the Covenant at Sinai together with the Children of Noah's Covenant; that is to say, people recognizing that the God who Created Heavens and Earth is also the *King of the World*, thus establishing precepts (*miṣvot*) for Israel and the rest of humankind. As wrote Isaac Newton (1643-1727) in the 'General Scholium' to the *Principia*:

> *[W]e admire him (God) for his perfection; but we reverence and adore him on account of his dominion; for we adore him as his servants; and a god without dominion, providence, and final causes, is nothing else but Fate and Nature.*

Put in other words, a God without *miṣvot* which demand from his subjects *responsibility* and *accountability* "is nothing else but Fate and Nature."

Joseph Haddad has written a compelling book on the subject. It deserves to be *read* and *studied*.

JOSÉ FAUR
7 Tammuz, 5768
Netanaya, Israel

Have we not all one Father?

Did not one God create us [all]?

Why then is one person betrayed by another in order to defile the covenant of our forefathers?

[Malachi 2:10]

(The last of the Hebrew Prophets)

Introduction

As I write these words, the world is in the throes of tremendous conflict. Implacable foes of the United States and the Free World are at the cusp of acquiring nuclear weapons. We may loosely characterize the 20th century as a battle between the forces of fascism and communism versus democracy and capitalism. World Wars I and II were fought over the rising power of tyrants, empowered in young nation-states, who sought world domination. Communism aspired to redistribute wealth in a newly industrialized and socially-conscious world order. The defeat of the Axis powers in World War II and the disintegration of the Soviet Union in the late 20th century heralded the triumph of Democracy and Capitalism.

At the close of the 20th century, the family of nations seemed to embrace the values of democracy (as the ideal form of government) and capitalism (as the preferred economic format). However, the early part of the 21st century has witnessed the collapse of the financial underpinnings of the capitalist mode. Unbridled capitalism has brought about tremendous dislocation and the current financial crisis portends a serious and protracted worldwide depression. While democracy, the notion that each individual be given an equal voice in determining the nature of government is most appealing, it too has its limitations and dangers. No better example of what Thomas Jefferson characterized as the "tyranny of democracy" is needed than Nazi Germany. Hitler came to power through democratic elections, and the anti-Jewish legislation that culminated in the horrors of the Holocaust were "enacted by the majority" in Germany.

Amidst this global instability the age-old issue of religiously motivated warfare, simmering in the final quarter of the 20th century has re-emerged with full force in the early part of the 21st century, posing a dire threat to mankind's stability. The belief in a benevolent Creator of the world should ostensibly promote peace and harmony. However, religious beliefs are subject to development and distortion, with interpretations of God and what he expects of Man differing vastly — with tragic consequences. Many ask: What kind of benevolent God would ask of his believers to offer their lives in order to destroy innocent men, women, and children of another faith or even another sect within the same faith community?

The purpose of this work is to share a truth that is too often overlooked and misunderstood. While simple, it is sublime:

We are indeed all God's children.

Though we may have different languages, cultures, beliefs, and faiths, human beings remain fundamentally related to each other, members of an extended family. This message is fundamental to the Bible, accompanied by a prescription for perfecting oneself as an individual, a member of a community, a nation, and ultimately as a member of all of humanity.

We desperately need to reexamine the common threads of our humanity, before it is too late. The Bible begins its message by depicting the story of the creation of the cosmos, culminating with Man, the "crown of creation." Man is created as God's most noble creature, realized in Man's singular capacity for exercising free-will. A careful reading of Genesis will provide us with a paradigmatic series of events through which we can follow the development of man. Man is born, full of opportunities and splendid potential, subsequently squandered through his choices and their consequences.

After a series of abysmal events, a "giant of a man," Abraham, begins the arduous process of showing mankind the return to the blissful existence from which we were banished. Abraham fathers what are to later be called the children of Israel, the Jewish people. Abraham began a tradition of acting with justice and righteousness and transmitted this notion to a people who would herald this as the hallmark of their society, promulgating the idea of ethical monotheism to the rest of the world

Judaism, the heir of the Abrahamic legacy, encompasses a faith-community that embraces a common genealogical people, as well as any and all who elect to join. Unlike the common misconception that Judaism is a race that originated from a single ethnic source, Judaism is comprised of the members of each and every race who subsequently embraced the truths and mission of the Jewish tradition. History is replete with outstanding personalities amongst the Jewish people who were proselytes or children of proselytes. The hope of this work to reawaken the awareness of our shared origin and potential for grandeur, as well as our all-too-human frailties; and to underscore that we are, for better or for worse, inextricably interrelated.

Reading the Bible

If literature is the written expression of the human spirit, then the Hebrew Bible is the written expression of the Divine spirit. The Infinite constrained his wisdom, so to speak, in the shape and form of the Bible. An ancient Jewish teaching holds that the script of the Bible – from the first letter *"bet"* of the book of Genesis to the final letter *"lamed* "in the book of Deuteronomy – is one long name of God.[1] The entire corpus of the Five Books of Moses are an interrelated whole, containing the essence of Divine wisdom and counsel for mankind.

This gift, embodied in the Decalogue and culminating in the Hebrew Bible, is a formula designed to help humanity transcend its ills. The Decalogue (commonly mistranslated as the "Ten Commandments") is comprised not of ten commandments but rather ten principles, which provide an outline for what the Jewish tradition counts as 613 biblical commandments. This unique theophany at Sinai, where Moses and the entire nation experienced a profound prophecy, marked the beginning of the written text of the Bible. Moses subsequently underwent many prophetic encounters in the Tabernacle, which was a portable Temple assembled and disassembled periodically throughout the Israelites' early history. It was from that place that he faithfully scribed the text of what was to be the first five books of the Hebrew Bible, also known as the Five Books of Moses.[2]

Named after the Greek *biblos,* meaning "book," the Hebrew Bible is indeed just that: the Book of Books. This best-selling volume of all time may be studied from a number of perspectives such as comparative history or linguistics. From a literary point of view, the Bible includes various forms of writing, such as simple prose, satire, irony, and poetry, yet these perspectives, though important, are ancillary and only incidental to the Bible's primary message. The Sages of the Hebrew Bible, transmitters of the biblical tradition, teach that the Biblical text penned by Moses as a faithful scribe from the Divine author, is pregnant with multi-layered levels of meaning. No dot or title is without is significance.[3]

A major principle in understanding Biblical law is the relationship between the Written and Oral law. This Oral law is a tradition of explanations and methods of understanding in which the Biblical law is applied to every issue and problem that arises, without which an understanding of the Written Law would be incomplete. This very rich and elaborate legal tradition, beginning with seventy elders appointed by Moses and ratified by God through a prophetic encounter, evolved into a phenomena that explained, applied, and developed biblical law into each and every sphere of life, identifying each and every contingency possible.

This process culminated in the redaction of the main corpus of Oral law known as the Talmud in approximately 600 C.E. The Talmud is an encyclopedic collection of legal analysis and moral reflection that was developed over hundreds of years on every aspect of society and life, framed primarily by the scholars, jurists, and disciples who headed the Sanhedrin. After its publication, the Talmud spawned literally hundreds if not thousands of legal responsa as well as further collections of analysis and commentary, that continue to this day.

The Bible's purpose is to teach us about Man and God, and in so doing, to provide us with a moral and legislative code with which to guide our lives, in both a universal and particularistic way. The family of Man is enjoined to live their lives in a certain manner, while the children of Abraham, Isaac, and Jacob are called upon to conduct their lives according to a highly-structured format, serving as teachers and role models for their fellow human beings.

The narrative portion of the Five Books of Moses tells the story of Abraham and his children, where we mark the transition from a family, to a tribal group, to a nation. After the story of Creation, we have a series of four narratives that speak of the dawn of human society, together forming a paradigm of early man and his failures. They may be summarized as follows: (1) Adam and Eve in the Garden of Eden, (2) Cain and Abel, (3) Noah and the Deluge, (4) The Tower of Babel. Rather than mere historical accounts of a lost era, we are meant to seek within them the means by which humanity can rise above repeated catastrophe and redeem ourselves.

Learning from Creation

In the beginning God created heaven and earth. The earth was without form and empty, with darkness on the face of the depths, but God's spirit moved on the water's surface. God said, 'There shall be light' and light came into existence. God saw that the light was good and God divided between the light and the darkness. God named the light 'day,' and the darkness he named 'night.' It was evening and it was morning: one day.

[Genesis 1:1-5]

God said, "The earth shall bring forth particular species of living creatures, particular species of livestock, land animals, and beasts of the earth." It happened. God thus made particular species of beasts of the earth, particular species of livestock, and particular species of animals that walk the land. God saw that it was good. God said, "Let us make Man with our image and likeness. Let him dominate the fish of the sea, the birds of the sky, the earth." God thus created man with his image, in the image of God he created him, male and female he created them. God blessed them. God said to them, "Be faithful and become many. Fill the land and conquer it. Dominate the fish of the sea, the birds of the sky, and every beast that walks the land.

[Genesis 1:24-29]

The Bible describes the Creation story from day one through day six in prose that, in its simplicity, is intelligible to a young child, while simultaneously obscuring layers of meaning that continue to awe the most sophisticated minds. Modern cosmologists are only beginning to appreciate the profundity of the Biblical creation narrative.

Indeed, some contemporary physicists have made discoveries corroborating the creation story as depicted in the Bible. Physicist Dr. Gerald Schroeder tackles the seeming contradiction between the biblical narrative of the creation occurring in six days and most modern cosmological estimations in his brilliant work *Genesis and the Big Bang* which approximate the development of the universe over a period of some 15 billion years from the initial "big bang." Based on Einstein's theory of relativity, Schroeder maintains that time actually dilates based on the perspective of the observer. He writes:

> *In the first six days of our universe's existence, the Eternal clock saw 144 hours pass. We know now that this quantity of time need not bear similarity to time passed as measured in another part of the universe. As dwellers within the universe, we estimate the passage of time with clocks found in our particular placement, and measurements of rates and distances in an expanding universe. It is with these clocks that humanity travels. When the Bible describes the day by day development of our universe on the six days following the creation, it is truly referring to six 24 hour days. But the reference frame by which those days were measured was one which contained the total universe.*[4]

Another renowned scholar, Dr. Nathan Aviezer, chairman of the Department of Physics at Bar Ilan University, explains the story of creation as propounded in the Bible, against the backdrop of the most current science. In his work, *In the Beginning: Biblical Creation and Science,* Dr. Aviezer makes a compelling analysis of the biblical text as describing creation in concurrence with modern scientific inquiry. Unable to solve the riddle of the formation of life, scientists today remain mystified concerning the sudden appearance of living organisms. Dr. Aviezer explains that this perplexity is borne out by current fossil evidence, in which there is little pointing to a gradual evolution of life. However, he sees no inconsistencies between the biblical narrative and the idea that livings organisms were formed of inanimate matter.[5] The "central dogma of molecular biology," highlighting what scientists call the "paradox of the origin of life," cannot trace the evolution of how the very first nucleic acids, which produced the proteins necessary for living cells were created; leaving the possibility that they must have spontaneously developed from inanimate matter.[6]

In the Biblical text, this fact is accounted for with the unique usage of the verb *bara* (meaning "created") in the account of the formation of great sea creatures on the fifth day of creation. This verb, as opposed to other seeming synonyms, is used only rarely in the creation story; first with the inception of creation in the first verse of the first chapter, and lastly with the creation of man on the sixth day. This instance of *bara*, the second of three in the creation narrative, heralds a being that is not a mere re-working of prior elements, but something entirely new. The wording of the Bible here connotes that the creation of animal life is, conceptually, a wholly new creation.

Dr Aviezer reaches the following conclusion:

> *In reference to the first animals the biblical expression "God created" denotes the transformation of inanimate matter into living organisms. Indeed, this divinely directed transformation resulted in an entity whose properties are so utterly different from the original inanimate matter that no verb other than "created" seems adequate to describe the change.*[7]

Much has been written in recent years attesting to the fact that a serious scientific approach need not contradict the Bible's account of creation. However, we need not necessarily search for ways in which to conflate the two accounts of creation. Rather, it may very well be that the two exist in entirely different realms. Science is an attempt to comprehend the "how" of creation: how we and the world we inhabit came to be and continue to exist. The Bible, on the other hand, concerns itself with the "why" of creation, the issue of where we are headed.

Why are we here? Where are we headed? A serious reading of the book of Genesis will help us understand the answer to these questions.

In the Garden

The Bible concludes the account of creation of the world with the creation of Man on the sixth day. The Bible is very explicit in using the Hebrew verb *bara* (created), as opposed to the other verbs used in the Biblical creation narrative, such as *yatzar* (formed) or *asa* (made). This term is also used to describe the first animal life in the fifth day account as noted above, as well as the radical creation of Heaven and Earth in the very first verse of the Bible. When man is created, he is heralded as a new being, unprecedented in prior creation. Unlike the other creations both inanimate and animate, only man is created in the image of God:

> *God said, "Let us make Man with our image and likeness, let him dominate the fish of the sea, the birds of the sky, the livestock animals, and all the earth and every land animal that walks the earth." God thus created man with his image. In the image of God he created him, male and female he created them.*
>
> [Genesis 1:26-28]

Man's uniqueness is born of his composite nature, at once made of the dust of the earth which provides his physical form, while simultaneously infused with the "breath of God," a creative free-willed capacity. Man is the ultimate "sui-generis," both matter and spirit, body and soul. Most Rabbinic commentators describe this special capacity of mankind as the capability of recognizing God as well as the capacity for self-awareness.

Mankind was also blessed with the tool to express this recognition: the gift of speech.

> *God took the man and placed him in the Garden of Eden to work it and watch it. God gave the man a commandment saying, "You may eat from every tree of the garden. But from the 'Tree of Knowledge of Good*

and Evil,' do not eat, for on the day you eat from it, you will definitely die.

[Genesis 2:5-17]

New man is entrusted with a seemingly simple charge; what could be so easy as to refrain from partaking of the Tree of Knowledge? What a blissful existence! Man and woman were blessed together with every delight at their disposal, yet they could not restrain themselves. Urged by the serpent, a manifestation of curiosity and temptation, they disobey and partake of the forbidden fruit. Thereupon they gain the knowledge of the difference between good and evil; following God's will or thwarting it. Man however, seeks to rationalize his actions, described as "a means to gain enlightenment" (Genesis 3:6). Upon partaking of the fruit and uncovering their actions, Man then seeks to justify his decision, passing the buck, so to speak; Adam blames the woman and Eve blames the serpent. (Genesis 3:8)

This episode becomes a paradigm for an individual's sin for all time. Man, curious creature that he is, is tempted by his desires. He rationalizes his actions and seeks to justify himself at the expense of others. Placing himself as the center of authority, he sins. Through sinning against God, Man also distances himself from his fellow. The act of sin creates a chasm between Man and those closest to him, Eve, whom Adam knew to be the "bone from my bones and flesh from my flesh" (Genesis 2:23). The resolution of estrangement between man and his fellow, and man and God is the Bible's objective, its hope for humanity.

Brother's Keeper

The theme of man's estrangement from his fellow continues into the next major episode of Genesis. Upon banishment from the blissful material life in the Garden of Eden, Adam begets twins and the earth is divided in two. Cain becomes a farmer, tilling the soil, and his brother Abel becomes a shepherd. Both seek to offer of their possessions a thanksgiving to God, a gesture of obeisance, gratitude, yet one brother's offering is flawed:

> *An era ended. Cain brought some of his crops as an offering to God. Abel also brought some of his firstborn of his flock, from his fattest ones. God paid heed to Abel and his offering but to Cain and his offering, he paid no heed. Cain became furious and depressed.*
>
> [Genesis 4:3-6]

Apparently Abel's offering, unlike his brother Cain's, is marked by its superior quality, an indication of genuine gratitude to God rather than something perfunctory. Cain's displeasure at the acceptance of his brother's offering even while God rejects his own, is addressed by God, who urges him to understand that all is not lost, that the opportunity for self-improvement still exists. Cain is urged to sublimate these tendencies toward jealousy and anger towards improving his character, presenting man with the opportunity to change, to grow.

> *Cain said something to his brother Abel. Then, when they happened to be in the field, Cain rose up against his brother Abel and killed him. God asked Cain, "Where is your brother Abel?" "I do not know," replied Cain, "Am I my brother's keeper?" God said, "What have you done? The voice of your brother's blood is screaming to Me from the ground [...] When you work the ground, it will no longer give you of its strength. You will be restless and isolated in the world."*

> *Cain said, "My sin is too great to bear! Behold, today you have banished me from the face of the earth and I am to be hidden from Your face. I am to be restless and isolated in the world, and whoever finds me will kill me."[...] Cain went out from before God's presence.*
>
> [Genesis 4: 8-14]

We are not told by the Biblical narrator what it is that Cain said to his brother. However, it is clear that God's previous admonition to Cain is not heeded. Cain, seething with jealousy, waits for the right opportunity– and when it arises, callously murders his brother. Cain is thus condemned to suffer the consequences of his actions, restless and isolated in the world. He is ostracized from society and forfeits his proximity to the Divine presence. Whereas Adam presented us with a paradigm of individual sinning against his Creator, this time man sins against his fellow man, his very own brother. Man is the quintessential social being. Given the gift of speech and with the ability to recognize his creator, he also communicates with his fellow man. Each human is able to recognize each other's uniqueness, something impossible in the animal world. Each is able to share – thoughts feelings, hopes, dreams. This is the source of man's overcoming his sense of loneliness. And man's loneliness is a product of his uniqueness. When one human kills another he violates and negates the essence of his own humanity. In so doing he destroys his own Godliness. When Cain kills his brother Abel, fraternity is destroyed, the mutual recognition and shared sense of uniqueness is lost. Man is no longer human.

Noah and the Deluge

Humanity procreates and the generations continue. Mankind multiplies and society is formed. However,

> *God saw that Man's wickedness on earth was increasing. Every impulse of his innermost thought was only for evil, all day long [...] God said, "I will obliterate humanity that I have created from the face of the earth - Man, livestock, land animals, and birds of the sky. I regret that I created them." But Noah found favor in God's eyes [...] The world was corrupt before God and the land was filled with crime. God saw the world and it was corrupted. All flesh had perverted its way on the earth. God said to Noah, "The end of all flesh has come before Me. The world is filled with [Man's] crime. I will therefore destroy them with the earth."*
>
> [Genesis 6:5-13]

The story of Noah and the flood can be seen as the prime example of collective Man sinning against his brother, a crime so grave in the eyes of God, that it compromises the entire world's right to existence. The Bible uses distinct language to paint the extent of the moral depravity which had pervaded Noah's society. "Corruption" (Hebrew *shachat*), has the connotation of decadence, perversion, destruction, and damage, especially used to denote sexual immorality and idolatry. "Crime" (Hebrew *chamas*) refers to more violent forms of action, characterized by oppression, cruelty, and outrage. The consequences were inevitable; society could not persist. In a poignant passage, God anthropomorphically "regretted that he had made Man on earth and was pained to his very core" (Genesis 6:6). The creation which God referred to on the sixth day as "very good" had now been perverted by man, the supposed "crown" of his work.

Noah, however, with his immediate family, was to be spared. Society is destroyed, collective Man fails, but the family unit persists and is the only hope left for man. By cruelly sinning against his fellow man, society lost its right to exist. Noah, by virtue of his righteousness, is able to save himself and his family, and the future of humanity along with them. The turbulent floodwaters obliterate the rest of humanity together with all living land creatures. The earth is cleansed of pollution; all vestiges of a corrupted society are washed away. Upon leaving the ark to a ravaged earth Noah becomes a second Adam, father to all humanity.

God makes a promise to humanity through Noah, that the earth will never again be destroyed by flood. The rainbow becomes the sign of this covenant (Genesis 9:9-11). Indeed it is the ideal natural metaphor; the rainbow shines when the rainfall ceases, a reminder that never again shall the heavenly waters pour without end.

Despite the promise, Noah finds himself depressed and dejected from the experience of returning from the ark to a barren, lifeless earth.

> *Noah began to be a man of the soil, and he planted a vineyard. He drank some of the wine, making himself drunk, and uncovered himself in the tent. Ham, the father of Canaan, saw his father naked, and he told it to his two brothers outside. Shem and Japheth took a cloak and placed it on both their shoulders. Walking backwards, they then covered their father's nakedness. They faced away from him and did not see their father naked. Noah awoke from his wine-induced sleep, and he realized what his youngest son had done to him. He said, "Cursed is Canaan! He shall be a slave's slave to his brothers!" He then said, "Blessed be God, the Lord of Shem! Canaan shall be his slave! May God expand Japheth, but may he dwell in the tents of Shem. Let Canaan be their slave!"*
>
> [Genesis 9:20]

What Ham, or Canaan, does to Noah within the confines of the tent is not explicitly stated. Biblical verse generally uses the term "uncover the nakedness" as a euphemism for sexual relations. That Ham or Canaan committed a homosexual act or perhaps castrated Noah are possibilities entertained by traditional Biblical commentators. Suffice it to say that Noah's drunken stupor was seen in a negative light. The subsequent promiscuous act of Noah's son, or grandson, suggests that Ham or Canaan did not want Noah to further procreate, leaving the rest of the earth's riches to be divided by Noah's three sons. Indeed, Noah, through his three sons, becomes the second father of humanity. The generations following Noah, Japheth, Ham, and Shem, continuing through Peleg, son of Eber, number seventy in all. These become what are later known in Talmudic tradition as the seventy nations of the world.

The Tower of Babel: Falling Apart

The entire earth had one language with uniform words. When the people migrated from the east, they found a valley in the land of Shinar, and they settled there. They said to one another, "Come let us mold bricks and fire them." They then had bricks to use as stone and asphalt for mortar. They said, "Come let us build ourselves a city and a tower whose top shall reach the sky. Let us make ourselves a name, so that we will not be scattered all over the face of the earth." God descended to see the city and the tower that the sons of mankind had built. God said, "They are a single people, all having one language, and this is the first thing they do! Now nothing they plan to do will be unattainable for them! Come let us descend and confuse their speech, so that one person will not understand another's speech." From that place, God scattered them all over the face of the earth, and they stopped building the city. He named it Babel, because this was the place where God confused the world's language. It was from there that God dispersed [humanity] over all the face of earth."

[Genesis 11:1-8]

In this brief fourth and final narrative prior to the emergence of Abraham, mankind is united in a perverse unity. Man bands together in challenging God, intending to build a tower "whose top shall reach the sky" (Genesis 11:5). In a massive biblical understatement, the text does not explain the exact nature of the sin of this generation. It does not have to. This perverse project of Man's self-aggrandizement needs no further elaboration. The society that arose in Shinar resembled Communism, though predating it by thousands of years. "Man" collectively became the object of self-worship. Each individual had no value; only the "project" mattered. Traditional biblical commentators, in describing the building of the tower, relate that if a single brick fell, the workers would lament the loss of time and productivity. However, if a worker fell to his death, no one would care.[8] The individual man was irrelevant and worthless compared to the deified collective Man.

Though unity is important and can be positive, it is only so if the individuals who comprise that unity are respected. Without respect for the individual, unity for its own sake becomes a form of idolatry, turning Man into a god. Single-minded opinion, expressed through a single solitary language, forces conformity, perverting the original meaning of what it is that makes us created in God's image. That Godly image implies the diversity and unique makeup of each and every individual. In seeking to supplant God, Man forfeits the essence of his own humanity – that unique part of each and every individual that defines us as being created in God's image. As a result, mankind is dispersed to the four corners of the earth. God confounds Man's ability to communicate by forcing upon him multiple languages. He will have to very slowly learn how to reunite with his fellow.

Reviewing these four stories, it seems we have seen nothing but early Man's repeated failures. The story of "Adam and Eve in the Garden of Eden" represents individual Man sinning against God. "Cain and Abel" is a tale of the individual man sinning against his fellow man. "Noah and the Deluge" presents the errors of collective Man – society— sinning against his fellow man, and finally "The Tower of Babel" represents collective Man, i.e. society, sinning against God. It seems the human condition is doomed to failure. Repeatedly, Man cannot rise above his pettiness and ego, both on an individual basis and on a collective societal basis. He fails with respect to his fellow man and he fails with respect to his relationship with God. Though Noah was a great individual, he was unable to save anybody outside his immediate family. Only an individual like Abraham was able to chart a different path, the long and difficult journey to redemption. It is a path he began, and one that his children still take; and it is the subject of the Biblical story.

The Noahide Laws: Universal Law of Humanity

Put very simply, Man's responsibility as the child of God is to lead his life properly; to give an accounting to God and his fellow man, both as an individual and as a member of society. This entails accepting the notion which ultimately became the bedrock for the society which would come to dominate the world; that is, to acknowledge that "all men are created equal," in God's image. As such, Man has a responsibility to himself, to his fellow, and to society as a whole.

What exactly does God want of Man? He wants Man to be a "child of Noah" (Hebrew *ben Noah*), or in the popular Yiddish expression, a "*mentsch*"— a decent human being. The Bible and Jewish tradition teach that all of mankind is to live by seven basic laws of morality, known as the seven Noahide principles. Rather than serving as a primitive list of regulations for ancient Man, these principles, may serve as a compelling guideline for human action in the 21st Century, giving form and structure to the relativistic notions of morality. There is no doubt that the legal system developed by Western society, with its emphasis on expanded human rights and concern for the less fortunate members of society, has its basis in the seven Noahide principles outlined in the book of Genesis. These precepts are: (1) The prohibition against idolatry, which entails monotheism - the belief that there is one Creator who fashioned the universe and is concerned with his creation; (2) The prohibition against blasphemy, a regulation which defines how one may relate to the Divine, forbidding desecration of the Divine name; (3) The prohibition against murder; (4) The prohibition against sexual immorality; (5) The prohibition against theft; (6) The prohibition against eating from a living animal, which is a fundamental notion opposing excessive cruelty; and (7) the requirement to establish courts of justice.

With the exception of the directive to establish courts of justice, all formulations are made in the negative. Why this list of prohibitions? The answer lies in the fact that the Creator wants to give Man the maximum amount of flexibility possible to behave as he sees fit. The basic limitations of these negative prohibitions, which serve as a guideline for basic morality, provide Man with the maximum amount of flexibility, granting him the liberty to make his own choices. In contrast, the Jewish people are given a total of 613 biblical precepts; however, through a discussion of the ramifications of these seven principles, we will see that the initial disparity is not as great as the numbers seem to imply.

The Prohibition Against Idolatry: In Support of Monotheism

"Do not have any other gods before Me."

[Exodus 20:3]

Fundamental to Man's efforts in establishing a just and equitable society is the idea that there exists one benevolent Creator, who not only formed the cosmos but also cares about his creation. This realization implies that no worship of anything other than the one unified Creator can be tolerated. Thinking people throughout the ages have attempted to "prove" the existence of God. Many have noted that "proof" of God in the objective sense of the word does not exist in our world, where the option of rejecting God's existence must exist as a ballast to free will. Those individuals, who believe the only measure of truth is that which is objectively quantifiable, will by their own definitions have ruled out the existence of a Being who is necessarily Supra-rational. Nevertheless, we will briefly review some of the more popular classical proofs providing intellectual pathways to conceptualizing the idea of God's existence.

The Ontological Proof

First formulated by St. Anselm (1033-1109), the archbishop of Canterbury, this proof revolves around the definition of God as something of which nothing greater can be conceived. By "greater" he does not mean something spatially larger, but rather superior or more perfect. Since "reality" is superior to "non-reality" it follows that the most perfect and superior of conceptions must be a reality that indeed does exist. This "reality" is worthy of our obeisance and worship and it is what we call God.

The Cosmological Argument

This argument refers to a proof based around the notion of the "First Cause" or "Primary Mover" formulated by the great Greek philosopher Plato (428-348 BCE) in his famous dialogues. Plato's argument begins with the premise that the power to produce movement is logically prior to the power to receive and pass on movement. In order for there to be "causes" undergoing and transmitting change, there must be an "uncaused cause" to originate the movement. The only kind of reality with the power of spontaneous movement is a "soul"; therefore, the ultimate cause of a universe in motion must be a living "soul." More simply, Plato extends the notion to the simple observation that everything that we experience has something which precedes it, which caused it to happen. That First Cause, before which there was no previous cause, is God.

The Teleological Argument

Like the cosmological argument, the teleological argument, also known as "the argument from design," is based on another premise intuitive to our notion of reality. When we encounter a watch (or any finely-designed precision instrument) found on the ground, we would never assume that the watch randomly "came to be." By its complexity, it exhibits design and we thereby conclude that the watch was fashioned by a watchmaker who created it with intent and purpose. The entire natural order, from the "macro" level of galaxy, solar, and planetary systems, to the "micro" level of cellular, atomic, and sub-atomic systems, displays unfathomable complexity and design. The "Grand Designer" of this immeasurably well-oiled machine, then, is God.

The Moral Argument

German philosopher Immanuel Kant sought to prove the existence of God not theistically, through pondering the origins of the universe, but rather through the origins of the baffling thing called the conscience, which points "to a supreme being as an implication of the fact of moral obligation, an implicate that is unavoidable by anyone who acknowledges obligation as having an absolute and unconditional authority over him." Kant presupposes the existence of the idea of the highest good *summom bonum*, an intrinsically valuable state of affairs which a moral being must want to establish or promote to such an extent as is within his power. Accordingly, it is our character as moral agents, acknowledging the commands of duty and believing in the ultimate "realizability" of the highest good, to assume or postulate the existence of God, to whom we are beholden. From where else could the desire for the abstract "good" rather than the most expedient spring forth? For Kant, God is the summit of our motivation for doing the right or moral thing.

Proof from Religious Experience

As we have said before, the classical proofs, several of which we have summarized here, provide sufficient "proof" of God's existence— for the believer. For the skeptic, agnostic, or atheist, however, many theoretical counter-arguments have been proposed, sophisticated and possibly convincing. However, the believer does not require comprehensive logical proof to assert the existence of God and alternatively, for the non-believer or skeptic, no amount of logical proof will suffice. For many, what provides overwhelming evidence of the existence of God is direct experience of the Divine. Seeking logical demonstrations of God's reality is superfluous for those aware of His presence on a personal and intimate level.

Awareness of God, our ability to experience his presence, takes many forms, from our sensing the grand design in our contemplation of the beauty of a rose, or our sense of awe while gazing at a star-filled sky. It includes amazement and wonder in contemplating a newborn suckling its mother's breast or feeling, at times, God's presence when we are most alone and needy. Beyond the sense of awe and amazement, beyond the feeling of "creatureliness," we find the experience of meditative and mystical states. At the summit of religious experiences we have, for the perfected and gifted few, the prophetic experience.

No matter how it is accessed, the notion of God's existence and reality as the object of our worship is the bedrock of our humanity. Though we may scoff at the seemingly crude worship of stone images of a more ancient time, too many of us today worship the shallow emptiness of so many ephemeral images. Entertainment icons, rock stars, magnates, and moguls all project power, wealth, and sex. Are they not the idols of the modern day? When these personalities become our culture's heroes, does this not reflect a misguided notion of what is important in life? The face of idolatry take many forms, whether the mindless pursuit of instant gratification through drugs or alcohol, servile adulation of the latest film or music star, or the envy and awe reserved for the latest acquisition or conquest of the "corporate raiders." Indeed, the appellations of "idol" or "icon" which have become so common in our cultural lexicon, are accurate descriptions for these figures. Though the founding fathers of America spoke of certain "inalienable rights" to "life, liberty, and the pursuit of happiness," they did not mean a hedonistic pursuit of immediate pleasure, but rather the sense of accomplishment and true happiness acquired in a society that encourages liberty, religious freedom, economic opportunity, pluralism, and democracy.

The Prohibition Against Blasphemy: Reverence for the Divine

For a society to be truly just there must be a sense of reverence, a respect for what is hallowed. Ultimately, what is most holy, most sacred, is the Creator himself. As such, no profane speaking of God's name may be tolerated. This infraction is so serious that under certain circumstances the individual guilty of blasphemy is deserving of capital punishment, though in actuality, rabbinic courts were reluctant to exercise their biblical prerogative and rarely meted out this harsh sentence. The Bible prescribes capital punishment to highlight an offence it considers abhorrent and injurious to the proper functioning of society. In many instances, the written text of the Bible calls for capital punishment for the guilty party, but since the criteria for allowing the court to actually mete out a death sentence were so stringent, in actuality, it was virtually impossible to issue a verdict that incurred the death penalty. Before a death sentence could be meted out, a minimum of two proper witnesses were required to warn the pending offender that what he was doing was prohibited and that it was an offense punishable by death. A lack of one witnesses or complete warning could invalidate even the most seemingly straightforward case. Nevertheless, the Bible does record a case of public blasphemy whereby the offender received the death penalty, one of two cases in the Bible when a specific infraction by an individual occurs and the death penalty is the result:

> *The son of an Israelite woman and an Egyptian man went out among the Israelites, and the Israelite woman's son had a quarrel with an Israelite man in the camp. The Israelite woman's son then blasphemed God's name with a curse. [The people] brought him to Moses. His mother's name was Shelomith daughter of Divri, of the tribe of Dan. They kept him under custody until the penalty could be specified by God. God spoke to Moses saying: "Take the blasphemer out of the camp and let all who heard him place their hands on his head. The entire community shall then stone him to death. Speak to the Israelites as follows. Anyone who curses God shall bear his sin. But if one actually blasphemes the name YHWH, he shall be put to death. The entire community shall stone him."*
>
> [Leviticus 24:10-17]

Apparently, in the newly-established society that the Israelites formed in the desert, such a public desecration of God could not be tolerated. To do so would undermine the fabric of a society recovering from the slave mentality and idolatry of Egyptian culture. A society training to become arbiters of moral rectitude for the nations around them.

The Prohibition Against Murder

> *"Only of the blood of your own lives will I demand an account. I will demand an account from the hand of every wild beast. From the hand of man — even from*

> *the hand of a man's own brother — I will demand an account of every human life. He who spills human blood shall have his own blood spilled by man, for God made man with his own image."*
>
> [Genesis 9:5-7]

As we have stated, Man is created in God's "image." This endows infinite value upon his worth. Each human has the ability to view the world — indeed the entire cosmos — through the distinctive prism of his own perspective. It is no coincidence that the Sages propounded the view that "he who saves one human soul, it is as if he saved the entire universe. And he that takes one human soul it is as if he destroys the entire universe." This notion has become so ingrained in our thinking, that there is a scarcely a society today that does not prohibit murder in some form. However, the existence of relativistic notions of "acceptable" killings throughout the ages and cultures, phenomena such as duels, honor killings, ritualized suicide and euthanasia, prove that the "thou shall not murder" is not as obvious and intuitive an imperative as we may have initially thought.

The Prohibition Against Sexual Misconduct: Illicit Relations

Being free-willed creatures presupposes a series of regulations on the most intimate of human expressions, that of one's sexual conduct. Human relationships are meaningful and valuable. Judaism proposes that the most sacred of human relationships is the sexual union between a man and a woman, a union which creates not only physical, but spiritual and emotional oneness between two paradoxically incomplete wholes. As such, this union must not be with an "other" that is inappropriate. With this in mind, physical union must be performed between proper partners, precludes relations between certain blood relatives, individuals who have bound themselves to another through the marital union, or with non-humans. To father or mother a child is a beautiful and Godlike expression of creativity, an affirmation of faith in the further development and perfection of the world. When parenting a child, one partners not only with a significant other, but also with

God, so to speak. A prominent contemporary Jewish thinker, Rabbi Irving Greenberg, writes that having children after the Holocaust is a tremendous *mitzvah* (positive action). There is no greater statement which says that even after a Hitler, we believe that the world can still be a good place, than bringing a new life into the world.

Upon leaving the ark, Noah is told, "Be fruitful and multiply, and fill the earth." Though the Talmud does not reach a consensus about whether the command to procreate is included in the seven Noahide imperatives, a dissenting opinion sees it as an obligation for the "child of Noah" as well. In either case, the sexual union needs to be taken seriously and consummated with the proper partner. We have all seen how respecting the marital union is vital for the proper functioning of society. A disturbing phenomenon is now occurring in the gradual dissolution of the family unit in modern society. Many ills have resulted from the breakdown of the traditional family, and we must work to restore this sacred component of society to its proper status.

The Prohibition Against Theft

The prohibition against stealing is based on the simple premise that man is permitted to enjoy the fruits of his own labor, that to which God entitles him and prohibited from taking of that which is not his. To the Western mind, this precept seems almost simplistic.

For society to be just, proper regulations must be instituted to safeguard the personal property of the individual, which means outlawing all forms of illegal transfer of goods, whether stealing, robbery, cheating, craving another's property, repudiating debt, overcharging, withholding wages, or kidnapping. This notion is certainly a basic necessity for any society to function. Nevertheless, much of human history is filled with the unfortunate reality that an individual does not enjoy these rights when they conflict with the wishes of the king, sovereign or other government leadership.

The Prohibition Against Eating the Limb of an Living Animal

> *"There shall be a fear and dread of you instilled in all the wild beasts of the earth, and all of the birds of the sky, in all that will walk the land, and in all the fish of the sea. I have placed them in your hands. Every moving thing that lives shall be to you as food. Like plant vegetation, I have now given you everything. But nevertheless, you may not eat flesh of a living creature that is still alive."*
>
> [Genesis 9:2-4]

The formulation against eating a limb severed from a living animal, beast or fowl is one of basic human kindness and decency and is directed against cruelty to animals. For a man to be human, he is enjoined from cruelty even to those creations placed under his dominion, of that which he is allowed to take for his own consumption (permission which was given to Noah after he left the ark). The careful wording of "I have placed them in your hands" and "I have now given you everything" is the compelling source for Man not to abuse his mastery over the animal kingdom. The earth and all that it contains is placed in Man's hands, to utilize for his needs but also to preserve and nurture. We have begun to realize that the earth and all it contains comprise an interdependent ecological system. Man's standing at the head of the ecosystem gives him both privileges and responsibilities. We need to intelligently care for the earth and all it contains, for it has been "placed in our hands."

The Injunction To Establish Courts of Law: The Judicial System

The final of the seven Noahide precepts, the command to establish a legal system, is the only one formulated in the positive. The proper and healthy functioning of society is predicated on an institution that is designated by that society to legislate and enforce laws that are just and equitable. Though this imperative may seem vague in comparison to prior injunctions, according to scholar and Rabbi Aaron Lichtenstein, there are at least twenty biblical commandments implicit in the Noahide precept of justice.[20] These include the following commandments: (1) To appoint judges and officers in each and every community; (2) To treat litigants equally before the law; (3) To inquire diligently into the testimony of a witness; (4) To prohibit the miscarriage of justice by the court; (5) To prohibit the judge from accepting a bribe or gift from a litigant; (6) To prohibit a judge to show honor to a litigant; (7) To prohibit a judge from fearing threats from a litigant; (8) To prohibit a judge from compassionately favoring a poor litigant; (9) To prohibit a judge from discriminating against a litigant because he is a past sinner; (10) To prohibit a judge from mitigating a penalty due to excessive compassion; (11) To prohibit a judge discriminating against an orphan or alien; (12) To prohibit a judge from hearing one litigant in the absence of another; (13) To prohibit appointing a judge lacking knowledge of the law; (14) To prohibit the court from killing an innocent man; (15) To prohibit incriminating a party through circumstantial evidence; (16) To prohibit punishment for a crime committed under duress; (17) To execute the death penalty by the sword (decapitation); (18) To prohibit taking the law into ones own hands; (19) To testify in court; and (20) To prohibit false testimony.

Thus twenty of the 613 Mosaic biblical laws have application for the Noahide under the general precept to establish courts of justice. Professor Lichtenstein conducts similar studies with regard to the other Noahide principles, arriving at a total of sixty-six biblical precepts which directly apply to the Noahide system. Through this analysis Professor Lichtenstein demonstrates that the seven Noahide laws are much more than seven narrow pronouncements, but rather a system of extensive legislation narrating a moral way of life. The last (and only positive) precept establishes a judicial system that will decide any and all additional laws necessary and desirable for Man's continued development. The seven Noahide precepts are the basis for a system which is flexible and adaptable to man and society as mankind progresses.

This expanded legislation is the Bible's prescription for the Israelite model sovereign nation as well. The paradigm of the state of the children of Israel in their land of Israel is a model for humanity to establish in their respective sovereign lands The 613 biblical precepts for the Jew coalesce into a broad goal designed to create a society that will serve as a "kingdom of priests and a holy nation" (Exodus 19:6).

However, it is clear that many of the biblical precepts designed specifically for the Israelite nation are clearly ritualistic, providing extra "spiritual exercises" that are required for the expanded duties and responsibilities of the Jewish people. Just as an Olympic athlete is required to maintain an arduous training program to attain and maintain his peak athletic performance, so to the Jewish people, serving as mankind's priestly and holy "team," need to maintain a spiritual training program designed to keep them at maximum spiritual sensitivity. Just as an Olympic athlete adopts a strenuous and often grueling set of rules and regulations to keep him in top physical shape, regulating what he eats, exercising for long hours, and refraining from activities that may adversely affect his physical performance, so too the members of the Jewish "team" have a rigorous code that encompasses the way they eat, speak, and conduct all aspects of life. The seven basic principles for the family of man are enhanced into 613 complex precepts designed to keep the team of priests in top spiritual shape.

The system of justice that a particular society demands of itself sets the moral and ethical tenor of what it expects of its members. Only a society that places high value on the integrity and ethical comportment of its legal and judicial system can educate and improve itself. Indeed, these Biblical commandments are found to be the bedrock of all enlightened legal systems in today's modern world.

One such biblical precept which profoundly altered humanity is that of the Jubilee year (Leviticus 25:9-15). Throughout the Middle Ages and into the mid-nineteenth century, most of Western society was divided into strict classes. In an agricultural civilization, classes were divided between the landed gentry, those who made up the nobles and aristocrats, and the peasants or landless society who made up the lowest class. Feudalism, which characterized life from the ancient times until the dawn of the Industrial revolution, saw distinction between these classes. Landowners, despite offering protection and a meager income, often subjugated the commoners, taking a "lions share" of the produce.

In Biblical Israel, this was anathema. Upon entry into the promised land of Israel, each and every family of each and every tribe received its own inheritance, its own portion of land. By means of an elaborate lottery system, Joshua apportioned the land amongst the twelve tribes, to be passed down, through familial inheritance. If a person was for any reason reduced to poverty, he could sell his land to pay the debt. However all sales of inherited land in biblical Israel were in reality long-term leases. After a maximum of fifty years (seven cycles of seven sabbatical years), the land would revert back to its original owner in the fiftieth year, the Jubilee. An indigent person's land was restored to him, giving him a new start in life. A person who, for whatever reason, was reduced to poverty would be able to restore his dignity.

Three thousand years before social philosophers such as Locke, Rousseau, and Hobbes ever spoke of natural law, or about notions of equality and natural human rights, the Bible testifies:

> *"In the Jubilee year, every man shall return to his hereditary property. Thus when you buy or sell land to your neighbor, do not cheat one another. You are buying only according to the number of years after the jubilee; [therefore] he is selling it to you for the number of years that the land will produce crops [until the next Jubilee]. Since he is selling it to you for the number of crops, you must increase the price if it will be for many years, and decrease it if there are few. You will then not be cheating one another. You shall fear your God, since it is I who am God, your Lord. Keep my decrees and safeguard my laws. If you keep them, you will live in the land securely. The land will produce its fruit, and you will eat your fill, thus living securely in [the land]....Since the land is Mine, no land shall be sold permanently. You are foreigners and resident aliens as far as I am concerned and, therefore, there shall be a time of redemption for all your hereditary lands."*

[Leviticus 25:13-18, 23-25]

No individual could ever lord over another in Israelite society, for all are considered "foreigners and resident aliens," deriving rights from God's exclusive sovereignty.

Notions of social welfare, health care, educational opportunities, so widespread in modern progressive democracies all over Western Europe and the United States, stem from the Jubilee and other similar Biblical precepts. These are all examples of adapting the positive Noahide precept of setting up courts of Justice in order to do just that: establish justice for a particular society.

The Patriarchs: Abraham, Isaac and Jacob

How was Abraham different from his predecessors? He certainly was not the first monotheist. Adam, the first man, recognized his Creator; so did Cain and Abel. Indeed the Bible itself mentions a tradition of monotheists that included Seth and Enosh:

> *A son was born Seth and [Seth] named him Enosh. It was then initiated to pray with Gods name.*
>
> [Genesis 4:26]

This tradition continued through Noah:

> *Noah was righteous and walked with God.*
>
> [Genesis 5:9]

Abraham, to whom God reveals himself, instructs Abraham to

> *"Go away from your land, from your birthplace, and from your father's house, to the land that I will show you. I will make you into a great nation. I will bless you and make you great. You shall become a blessing. I will bless those who bless you and he who curses you, I will curse. All the families of the earth will be blessed through you."*
>
> [Genesis 12:1-4]

In a primitive tribal world, where every individual is identified with his home, Abraham is told to leave everything behind and chart a bold new course for himself. He is told that in so doing, he will become a source of blessing for all humankind. While Abraham was not the first monotheist, he was indeed the first to realize the ethical implications that knowledge of the Creator implied. If there is a Creator of heaven and earth, then that Creator must desire something from the created. This was, as the Bible describes, Abraham's distinction:

"I have given him special attention so that he will command his children and his household after him, and they will keep God's way, doing charity and justice."

[Genesis 18:19]

Not content to simply recognize his Creator, Abraham recognized that the Creator seeks of him, and all human beings, something more: the directive to act morally – to enact justice and righteousness.

Paradoxically, Abraham internalizes God's will to the extent that he dares to argue with God Himself. Unable to meekly accept God's declaration that he will destroy the wicked cities of Sodom and Gomorrah, Abraham proceeds to challenge the Creator himself! An amazing exchange ensues whereby a mortal man challenges and wrestles with his Creator. Abraham seeks to understand God's sense of justice. He pleads for some redeeming merit for the city.

"Will you actually wipe out the innocent together with the guilty? Suppose there are fifty innocent people in the city. Would you still destroy it, and not spare the place for the sake of the fifty good people inside it? It would be a sacrilege to ascribe this to you! Shall the whole world's Judge not act justly?"

[Genesis 18:23-26]

Humble, yet inquisitive, curious, and zealous to understand God's ways, Abraham's sense of justice presses him to go further.

Abraham spoke up and said, "I have already said too much before my Lord! I am mere dust and ashes!"

In a bizarre dialogue that appears to mimic an exchange at the bazaar, Abraham bargains with God, seeking mercy for the city if fifty, forty-five, forty, thirty, twenty, or ten, righteous people are to be found. It is for this passion for "justice and righteousness," which God recognized in Abraham, that Abraham merited being chosen by God. In reality, it was Abraham who chose God, however. Abraham sought to proclaim the passion for justice and righteousness, reflecting God's essence in every place he traveled, every person he met. The Bible gives a listing of the places

Abraham travels, not merely as a travelogue, but as a tribute to the work that Abraham carried forth in those places:

> *He [Abram] set up his tent with Bethel to the west and Ai to the east. He built an altar there and called in God's name.*
>
> [Genesis 12:7-8]

"Calling in God's name" refers to publicly affirming God's existence and proclaiming his dominion. Calling for allegiance and fidelity to the Creator, Abraham delivered the message that the Designer of the cosmos, despite being transcendent and unknowable, is also deeply imminent, caring, concerned and involved with the world. Abraham knew this to be true with his very being, for the fact that God let Abraham speak on behalf of the wicked people of Sodom, signified for Abraham that the Creator cares about Man's actions and that he is active in the world of Man.

Prior to sealing the decree against Sodom, the Bible recounts a remarkable passage:

> *"Shall I hide from Abraham what I am about to do? Abraham is about to become a great and mighty nation, and through him all the nations of the world will be blessed.*
>
> [Genesis 18:17-18]

In Abraham's sincerity in seeking to do what is just and right, God Himself, as it were, cannot withhold from him what He is about to do to Sodom. What Abraham was negotiating was a clear understanding of the possibility of redemption and reform for the population of Sodom. Would a group of fifty righteous individuals have the collective ability to inspire and persuade the wicked society to repent and mend their ways? At what point could or would one give-up trying to convince the people to do right?

The traditional commentators tell us that Sodom was a society depraved, bereft of any semblance of social welfare. Visitors were unwelcome and strangers unwanted. Lot, Abraham's nephew, lured to the verdant pastures of Sodom's locale was impressed with the possibility of a carefree and opulent lifestyle. Lot, no doubt positively influenced by the hospitality of his illustrious uncle, invites two guests into his home. Unknown to Lot, these strangers are angels, divine messengers-in-disguise, sent both to save him and his family and to destroy Sodom. Upon bringing these guests into his home, the city's populace quickly surrounds Lot's home, with the mob demanding the release of these strangers for their insidious desires.

Ironically, it is the very same Abraham, whom the narrative extols for possessing the quality of graciousness and hospitality, who argues on behalf of a society totally bereft of any semblance of those qualities. Finally Abraham is told that so small a group of ten righteous individuals would suffice as a nucleus to save Sodom from destruction, and yet there are not even that many. Thus assuaged, Abraham withdraws from his dialogue with God.

Abraham learns a vital lesson from this encounter with God. One man alone, no matter how noble or righteous, cannot as an individual redeem an entire society.

Abraham undeterred continues; and in a fascinating narrative of two instances of his travels, we learn volumes about his quest.

Abram's Call

Reviewing the lives of the patriarchs, we will concern ourselves with selected incidents in their lives that speak of the universal theme of their mission to spread ethical monotheism to the remainder of humanity. Undoubtedly all the Biblical stories have many ethical and moral lessons for us today. However the accounts of the patriarchs dazzle with their particular poignancy—as people having stature, character and nobility and at the same time human, with all too human failings. Their greatness lies in their sensitivity to the Divine calling within, their capacity for change and growth, which continue to inspire and inform us today.

No sooner then Abraham arrives in the land promised to him and his children, on a journey that entailed leaving everything he knew behind, then he is compelled to leave. The narrative continues:

> *There was a famine in the land. Abram headed south to Egypt to stay there for a while, since the famine had grown very severe in the land. As they approached Egypt, he said to his wife Sarai, "I realize that you are a good looking woman. When the Egyptians see you, they will assume that you are my wife and kill me, allowing you to live. If you would say that you are my sister. They will then be good to me for your sake, and through your efforts, my life will be spared." When Abram came to Egypt, the Egyptians saw that his wife was very beautiful. Pharaoh's officials saw her, and spoke highly of her to Pharaoh. The woman was taken to Pharaoh's palace. He treated Abram well because of her, and [Abram] acquired sheep, cattle, donkeys and male and female slaves, she-donkeys, and camels. God struck Pharaoh and his palace with severe plagues because of Abram's wife Sarai. Pharaoh summoned Abram and said, "How could you do this to me? Why*

didn't you tell me that she was your wife? Why did you say that she was your sister so that I should take her to myself as a wife? Now here is your wife! Take her and go!"

[Genesis 12:10-19]

Tellingly, an almost identical incident occurs once again to Abraham and Sarah, a few chapters later:

Abraham migrated from there to the land of the Negev, and he settled between Kadesh and Shur. He would often visit Gerar. [There] he announced that his wife Sarah was his sister, and Abimelekh, king of Gerar, sent messengers and took Sarah. God came to Abimelekh in a dream that night. "You will die because of the woman you took," He said, "She is already married." Abimelekh had not come near her. He said, "O Lord, will You even kill an innocent nation? Didn't [her husband] tell me that she was his sister? She also claimed that he was her brother. If I did something, it was with an innocent heart and clean hands." God said to him in the dream, "I also realize that you have done this with an innocent heart. That is why I prevented you from sinning against Me, not giving you the opportunity to touch her. Now return the man's wife, for he is a prophet. He will pray for you, and you will live. But if you do not return [her], you can be sure that you will die — you and all that is yours." Abimelekh got up early in the morning, and he summoned Abraham and said to him, "How could you do this to us? What terrible thing did I do to you that you brought such great guilt upon me and my people?" [...] Abraham replied, "I realized that the one thing missing here is the fear of God. I could be killed because of my wife. In any case, she really is my sister (also close relative)[...] When God made me wander from my father's house, I asked her to do me a favor. Wherever we came, she was to say that I was her brother." [...] Abimelekh said, "My whole land is before you. Settle wherever you see fit." To

Sarah he said, "I am giving your 'brother' a thousand pieces of silver. Let me be compensation for you and all who are with you for all that has been done. You can stand up tall." Abraham prayed to God, and God healed Abimelekh, as well as his wife and slave girls, so that they were able to have children. God had previously sealed up every womb in Abimelekh's house, because of Abraham's wife Sarah.

[Genesis 20:1-15]

The Bible, not known for verbosity, recounts this second very similar story of Sarah's abduction. In this case however, instead of sending away Abraham, as did Pharaoh, Abimelekh invites Abraham to stay and remain a part of his society. This difference is crucial in the Bible's attempt to instruct us about Abraham's – and his descendants' – future mission. Egypt was the world power. Its society was so alien to what Abraham was trying to teach, so entrenched in its pagan corruption, that it was as if Pharaoh had nothing in common with a man such as Abraham. He therefore needed to send Abraham away. Keeping so radical and prominent a personality such as Abraham in the midst of his Egyptian society would have been an affront to his rule and absolute authority. The great cosmopolitan center of Egypt had no place for an Abraham at that time. Abimelekh however, who was sovereign in a smaller, rural society was less hostile to Abraham's revolutionary ideas, revering him as a holy prophet. Pharaoh's abduction of Sarah, with its more sinister intent, brought about severe plagues to Pharaoh and his household. Abimelekh, whose intent was less malevolent, was punished with infertility, for him and his household.

In the less densely populated and semi nomadic atmosphere of Canaan the revolutionary ideas of Abraham were to be fertilized and take root. The idea of creating a society that recognized a single unified Creator and that this Creator had ethical and moral imperatives for man, needed this freedom to germinate. Abraham's task was to be incremental; slowly, deliberately, patiently he would inspire, educate, and affect all whom he and his descendants would come into contact.

Abraham's son Isaac, finally conceived when Sarah was ninety, was to follow in his footsteps. Ishmael, his son from his concubine Hagar, was not to share his father's aspirations and ideals.

> *The child grew and was weaned. Abraham made a great feast on the day that Isaac was weaned. But Sarah saw the son that Hagar had born to Abraham playing. She said to Abraham, "Drive away this slave together with her son. The son of this slave will not share the inheritance with my son Isaac!" This troubled Abraham very much because it involved his son. But God said to Abraham, "Do not be troubled because of the boy and your slave. Do everything that Sarah tells you. It is through Isaac that you will gain posterity. But still, I will also make the slave's son into a nation, for he is your child."*
>
> [Genesis 25: 8-13]

Even at this early stage, it is clear that Isaac is very different from his father Abraham. The Bible seems to describe him in a very passive manner. He is not the bold initiator as Abraham was, nor does he live the tumultuous and passionate life of his son and successor Jacob. Indeed the terse Biblical narrative that describes Isaac's life seems to repeat several events that occurred to Abraham.

The next major episode that occurs in Isaac's life is his own interaction with Abimelekh, king of Gerar. The two narratives, with their subtle differences, belie a different understanding of Isaac's mission, at once separate, and at the same time a continuation of his father's.

Isaac's Path

There was a famine in the land, aside from the first famine in the time of Abraham. Isaac went to Abimelekh king of the Philistines in Gerar. God appeared to [Isaac] and said, 'Do not go down to Egypt. Remain undisturbed in the land that I shall designate to you. Remain an immigrant in this land. I will be with you and bless you, since it will be to you and your offspring that I will give all these lands. I will thus keep the oath that I made to your father Abraham. I will make your descendants as numerous as the stars of the sky, and grant them all these lands. All the nations on earth shall be blessed through your descendants. All this is because Abraham obeyed My voice, and kept My charge, My commandments, My decrees, and My laws.' Isaac thus settled in Gerar. When the local men asked about his wife, he told them that she was his sister. He was afraid to say that she was his wife. Rebecca was so good-looking that the local men could have killed him because of her. Once, after [Isaac] had been there for some time, Abimelekh, king of the Philistines, was looking out the window, and he saw Isaac enjoying himself with his wife Rebecca. Abimelekh summoned Isaac.

'But she is your wife!' he said. 'How could you have said that she is your sister?'

'I was afraid that I would die because of her,' replied Isaac.

'What have you done to us?' demanded Abimelekh. 'One of the people could easily have slept with your wife! You would have made us commit a terrible crime!' Abimelekh issued an order to all the people: 'Whoever touches this man or his wife shall die!' Isaac farmed in

the area. That year, he reaped a hundred times [as much as he sowed], for God had blessed him. This was the beginning of his prosperity. He then continued to prosper until he became extremely wealthy. He had flocks of sheep, herds of cattle, and a large retinue of slaves. The Philistines became jealous of him. They plugged up all the wells that his father's servants had dug while Abraham was still alive, and they filled them with earth. Abimelekh said to Isaac, 'Go away from us. You have become much more powerful than we are.' Isaac left the area and camped in the Gerar valley, intending to settle there. He re-dug the wells that had been dug in the days of his father Abraham, which had been plugged up by the Philistines after Abraham's death. He gave them the same names that his father had given them. Isaac's servants then dug in the valley, and found a new well, brimming over with fresh water. The shepherds of Gerar disputed with Isaac's shepherds, claiming that the water was theirs. [Isaac] named the well Challenge [Esek], because they had challenged him. They dug another well, and it was also disputed. [Isaac] named it Accusation [Sitnah]. He then moved away from there and dug another well. This time it was not disputed, so he named it Wide Spaces [Rechovoth]. 'Now God will grant us wide open spaces,' he said, 'We can be fruitful in the land.' From there, [Isaac] went to Beersheba. God appeared to him that night and said, 'I am the God of your father Abraham. Do not be afraid, for I am with you. I will bless you and grant you very many descendants because of My servant Abraham.'

[Isaac] built an altar there and called in God's name. He set up his tents there, and his servants dug a well in the area.

[Genesis 26:1-25]

Here we see the Patriarch Isaac seemingly repeating what occurred to his father Abraham. In a time of famine however, God appears to Isaac and entreats him to remain in Canaan to enjoy and inherit his father's blessings. There was no possibility for Isaac to, in any positive way, affect Egyptian society. There was no place in Egypt for a child of Abraham. Isaac could do no more than repeat what his father had begun. Now, however, things were different in Canaan. Rebecca, Isaac's wife, was not taken to Abimelekh's home. The Bible carefully describes how Abimelekh, peering through his window, saw Isaac and Rebecca behaving as husband and wife. Only then does he realize that Rebecca is married. He then protests to Isaac, perhaps a bit disingenuously, that someone (no doubt he himself) might have taken Rebecca and sinned horribly.

We see that there is a pronounced improvement in the moral character of the local society between Abraham's first encounter with Abimelekh and Isaac's subsequent one, an improvement certainly to be attributed to Abraham's positive influence and teaching.

In another instance where the life of the father seems to chance upon his son, Isaac too digs many wells and also encounters conflict in their wake. Abraham, upon agreeing to establish a treaty with Abimelekh, had admonished the king about the well that "Abimelekh's servants had taken by force," a claim that Abimelekh fiercely denied (Genesis 21: 25-27). Isaac's servants re-dig Abraham's wells, which are subsequently plugged by Abimelekh's servants. In many ancient cultures, especially those lacking abundant water, the local well was the central focus of activity for both residents and wayfarers. Isaac builds an altar close to the well that he digs, reclaiming his father Abraham's message of ethical monotheism in the most visible location.

Yet the wells Isaac continues to build are repeatedly disputed. Both the physical wells and the message they represent are repeatedly blocked by Abimelekh's cronies. Finally, Isaac unearths a well that does not become a point of dispute.

Only at this point, after digging the third, undisputed well, does Isaac build the altar and call out in God's name. Rabbi Menachem Liebtag, contemporary Bible scholar, comments on these verses that only after the confrontation between Isaac and his neighbors had ceased, could Isaac proactively preach in God's name. In a fractious environment there was simply no one who would listen.[22]

The great medieval commentator, Nachmanides, suggests an intriguing idea concerning the wells, manifesting the greater biblical principle that "the actions of the fathers foreshadow those of the children." In this case, the desecrated wells of yore hint to the later building and destruction of the Temples in Jerusalem, destroyed in 587 B.C.E and 70 C.E respectively. The third well represents the Jewish tradition of the Third and final Temple of the Messianic era, an undisputed center of world spirituality providing spiritual nourishment and sustenance for all. The symbolism for Nachmanides is profound.

Once again, Abimelekh, seeing that God is with Isaac, seeks reconciliation through a treaty with Isaac. Both Abraham and Isaac, his successor, actively seek to introduce to pagan society the notion of a single Creator that demands of Man to live righteously. Poignantly, the biblical text follows Isaac's journey in the footsteps of his illustrious father, a process repeated continuously throughout the history of the Jewish people. This gradual introduction and reinforcement of morals and ethical behavior into larger society becomes the task of the Jewish people, set to continue to this very day.

Jacob's Ladder

The life of Jacob marks the end of the era of the Patriarchs. Rebecca, Isaac's wife and Jacob's mother, after a period of barrenness, finally conceives. The tumultuous conditions surrounding Jacob's birth foreshadow the trajectory of his less-than-peaceful life.

> *His wife was sterile, and Isaac pleaded with God for her sake. God granted his plea, and Rebecca became pregnant. But the children clashed inside her, and when this occurred, she asked, "Why is this happening to me?" Rebecca sought a message from God. God told her, "Two nations are in your womb. Two governments will separate from inside you. The upper hand will go from one government to the other. The greater one will serve the younger." When the time came for her to give birth, there were twins in her womb. The first one came out reddish, hairy as a fur coat. They named him Esau. His brother then emerged, and his hand was grasping Esau's heel. [Isaac] named him Jacob. Isaac was 60 years old when [Rebecca] gave birth to them. The boys grew up. Esau became a skilled trapper, a man of the field. Jacob was a scholarly man who remained with the tents. Isaac enjoyed eating Esau's game and favored him, but Rebecca favored Jacob.*
>
> [Genesis 25:21-28]

Esau, who would share none of his father's penchant for spirituality and outreach, becomes a skillful hunter. Jacob, "man of the tents," grows into a thinker and scholar. Isaac, sensing something missing in his own personality, enjoys the bounty of Esau's physical prowess and favors him. Rebecca, perspective and prophetic, sees the boys for their true natures and gravitates toward Jacob, whom she knows to be the only son fit to take over the mantle of Isaac's legacy.

Esau's brutish persona comes to the forefront in the callous manner by which he scorns the birthright—and the priestly duties that were meant as its accompaniment. Upon returning home from a grueling day of the hunt, Esau demands of Jacob:

> *"Give me a swallow of that red stuff, I'm famished!'"*
>
> *"First sell me your birthright," replied Jacob.*
>
> *"Here I'm about to die!" exclaimed Esau. "What good is a birthright to me?"*
>
> *"Make an oath to me right now," said Jacob. He made the oath, and sold his birthright to Jacob. Jacob then gave Esau bread and lentil stew. [Esau] ate it, drank, got up and left.*
>
> [Genesis 25:30-34]

This dichotomy between the brothers persists to the time that Isaac, elderly and sight-impaired, prepares to give his final blessing to his sons prior to his death. Isaac it appears, had in mind that both his sons would continue the legacy begun by his father Abraham; Esau providing the physical component needed to support the family's goals, while Jacob would develop the spiritual pursuits needed for the task on hand.

Rebecca, prophetically inspired by the experience of carrying two warring nations in her womb, knows that a partnership was not capable of lasting. She conspires to teach Isaac a lesson that will confirm her conviction. Rebecca cajoles Jacob into donning Esau's hunting cloak as she prepares a hearty venison meal for Jacob to present to Isaac, in her plan to have Jacob blessed (appropriately) under the guise of Esau. Isaac, subsequent to enjoying the feast, gives Jacob (thinking he is Esau) a blessing of material and temporal success. Already we see the glimmers of Rebecca's prophecy. Jacob adopts the more aggressive characteristics of his older brother, preparing him to bear the full brunt of his father's work later.

Needless to say, Esau is infuriated at Jacob for usurping his entitlement. As soon as the period of mourning is over, he makes plans to kill Jacob. Rebecca hears word of Esau's murderous intentions and advises Jacob to flee to her brother Laban in Charan, biding time for Esau's anger to subside. Rebecca presents her plan to Isaac as a suggestion for Jacob to seek a wife from her own hometown, rather than the pagan Hittite women of the land – an idea that Isaac finds agreeable (Genesis 27:41-46).

Prior to leaving for Charan to select a wife from Rebecca's hometown, Jacob is called in to bid farewell to his father. Isaac, realizing his former error in judgment, blesses Jacob again. This time he invokes not only a blessing for material success, but a far more wide-reaching blessing, calling forth Jacob's future role as builder of a great nation.

> *"God almighty will then bless you, make you fruitful, and increase your numbers. You will become an assembly of nations. He will grant Abraham's blessing to you and your descendants, so that you will take over the land which God gave to Abraham, where you previously lived only as a foreigner."*
>
> [Genesis 28:3-5]

On his solitary journey from his parents and home, Jacob's blessing from his father Isaac is corroborated by none other than the Almighty. Jacob has a vision: a ladder standing up on the ground, its top reaching heaven, angels ascending and descending.

> *Suddenly he saw God standing over him. God said, "I am the God, Lord of Abraham your father, and Lord of Isaac. I will give to you and your descendants the land upon which you are lying. Your descendants shall be like the dust of the earth. You shall spread out to the west, to the east, to the north, and to the south. All the families on earth will be blessed through you and your descendants. I am with you. I will protect you wherever you go and bring you back to this soil. I will not turn from you until I have fully kept his promise to you."*
>
> [Genesis 28:3-5]

Jacob's life is anything but tranquil, however. His natural inclination to be a "pure, whole scholar" did not characterize his eventful and difficult life (Genesis 25:27). Jacob earns the name "Israel," a name that means "he who struggles with man and God and prevails," an identity he bequeaths to a nation whose often tragic history mirrors that of its predecessor.

Jacob labors twenty years for his uncle Laban, who sets up the marriages of his daughters Leah and Rachel under false pretenses, betrothing Jacob to Leah first and requiring seven more years of labor to attain the beloved Rachel. Together with both his wives and two concubines, Bilhah and Zilpah, Jacob fathers eleven sons and a daughter. Despite Laban's constant trickery and subterfuge, Jacob grows exceedingly wealthy. Returning to his father's homeland with family and flocks, Jacob prepares to confront his nemesis and brother, Esau. Jacob is uncertain and terrified as his brother approaches his camp — accompanied by four hundred armed men.

> *Jacob was very frightened and distressed. He divided the people accompanying him into two camps, along with the sheep, cattle and camels. He said, "If Esau comes and attacks one camp, at least the other camp will survive." Jacob prayed: "O God of my father Abraham and God of my father Isaac. You Yourself told me, 'Return to the land where you were born, and I will make things go well with you.' I am unworthy of all the kindness and faith that you have shown me. [When I left home] I crossed the Jordan with [only] my staff, and now I have enough for two camps. Rescue me, I pray, from the hand of my brother— from the hand of Esau. I am afraid of him, for he can come and kill us all, mothers and children alike. You once said, 'I will make things go well with you, and make your descendants like the sand grains of the sea, which are too numerous to count.'"*
>
> [Genesis 32:8-13]

Jacob prepares and sends an impressive tribute of livestock and cattle, designed to win over his brother's good will. Then, in the middle of the night, Jacob sends his four wives and eleven children across the river shallows ahead. Upon completing the river crossing, Jacob finds himself alone and is suddenly assaulted by a mysterious stranger:

> *A stranger [appeared and] wrestled with him until just before daybreak. When [the stranger] saw that he could not defeat him, he touched the upper joint of [Jacob's] thigh. Jacob's hip joint became dislocated as he wrestled with [the stranger].*
>
> *"Let me leave!" said the stranger. "Dawn is breaking."*
>
> *"I will not let you leave unless you bless me."*
>
> *"What is your name?"*
>
> *"Jacob."*
>
> *"Your name will no longer be said to be Jacob, but Israel. You have become great before God and man. You have won."*
>
> *He then blessed [Jacob]. Jacob named the place "Divine Face."*
>
> *[He said,] "I have seen the Divine face to face, and my soul has withstood it."*
>
> [Genesis 32:27-33]

Jacob's nocturnal encounter with the mysterious stranger portends a defining moment in his life. Away from his father's home for so many years, riddled with doubt and guilt concerning his treatment of his brother, Jacob finally confronts his fears. Saddled with a large family and possessions, he seeks to protect them – all the while not knowing if his brother will be assuaged or vengeful. Commentators differ on the identity of this mysterious stranger. Some claim that he is the archangel of Esau, this struggle symbolic of many others in his past. Others see this struggle as a foreshadowing of the future, symbolic of an ongoing struggle against evil that would reflect Jacob's, and his children's, later efforts. Encompassing both ideas, we could say that Jacob struggled with his own inner doubts and temptations, haunted by remnants from the past threatening to shape his future.

Fortunately, Jacob is victorious, but the battle takes its toll, permanently debilitating Jacob's thigh. Jacob's spirit is renewed and he is renamed "Israel," meaning, in addition to its other previously mentioned denotation, "an officer of God."

Jacob and Esau finally meet and reconcile. Tactfully, Jacob suggests that Esau proceed on, as Jacob must cater to the tender pace of the children. They part on friendly terms.

Having returned to the land of Canaan with his entire family intact, Jacob doesn't have the privilege of enjoying a blissful life. Soon thereafter, his only daughter, Dinah, is abducted and raped by Shechem (son of the chief of the region, Chamor the Hivite) who proceeds to fall in love with Dinah and seeks to take her as a wife.

In a cunning ruse to rescue their sister, the sons of Jacob demand a price for Dina's hand: the circumcision of the entire male population of the town. Only then would they allow their sister, and future members of Jacob's family to intermarry with the town's population. Shechem convinces his fellow citizens to accept the offer. The men, including Chamor and Shechem, are all circumcised, anxious to win Dinah and acquire Jacob's wealth. On the third day of their circumcision, when the pain of circumcision is said to be the greatest, Simon and Levy, Dinah's brother's, come upon the city and rescue Dinah, slaying all the males of the city and plundering its wealth.

Jacob is horrified at this wanton killing. Although he appears to have tolerated the ruse designed to free his daughter, he did not expect this turn of events. Jacob confronts his sons:

> *Jacob said to Simon and Levi, "You have gotten me in trouble, giving me a bad reputation among the Canaanites and Perizites who live in the land. I have only a small number of men. They can band together and attack me, and my family and I will be wiped out."*
>
> *"Should he have been allowed to treat our sister like a prostitute?"*
>
> [Genesis 34:30-31]

The Hebrew phrase *achartem oti,* meaning "you have incriminated me," literally means "you have clouded/darkened me." Jacob castigates his two sons for "clouding up" the message that Jacob was trying to send to the people of Canaan. Circumcision, upon the very organ of reproduction, was to be a distinctive mark given to Abraham and his seed, the hallmark of the Jewish people. Here Jacob's sons connived, using this same mark of distinction, to free their sister, transforming the same organ that brought shame to Dinah to the organ that brought her freedom. Ironically, the townspeople sought to use this mark of distinction to assimilate into the family of Jacob, motivated by lust for Dinah and Jacob's wealth. Simon and Levi however, in taking revenge, not only free their sister but also kill all of the adult males of the city, also perverting the message of circumcision. Each side tragically uses the rite of circumcision for their own benefit.

In Jacob's eyes, this is not the message that he wants his family to proclaim. To his dying day, Jacob curses the anger of his sons Simon and Levi, bidding separation between these two hot-headed and passionate brothers.

Jacob and his family are commanded to flee to Beth El, but not before purifying themselves of any idolatrous artifacts from the Shechem looting. God protects the family, who escape unharmed by the people of Shechem and all the surrounding principalities. There, Jacob sets up an altar, returning to the very same place where, upon fleeing Canaan decades earlier, he had experienced his defining moment (Genesis 35:1-7).

At the very same spot, God again appears to Jacob, officially bestowing upon him the name of Israel, and granting him a vision of the nation that would carry his legacy:

> *"A nation and a community of nations will come into existence from you. Kings will be born from your loins. I will grant you the land that I gave to Abraham and Isaac. I will also give the land to you and your descendants who will follow you."*
>
> [Genesis 35:11-12]

Jacob is now complete as father of the children of Israel, crowned as the rightful spiritual heir to his father Isaac's and grandfather Abraham's legacy.

Tragically, Jacob's beloved wife Rachel dies in the throes of giving birth to Jacob's final son, Benjamin. Only Jacob amongst the Patriarchs succeeds in transferring the message of Man's ethical imperative to all of his children. Unlike Abraham, whose message was rejected by Ishmael; unlike Isaac, whose message was rejected by Esau; all of Jacob's children accept their mission of ethical responsibility. However, this family unity would not always be so apparent.

A Family Apart

The ability of the chosen family to influence the remainder of humanity in a positive manner is directly dependent upon the cohesion of the Children of Israel. Perhaps Jacob's family would also split among those who would follow the calling of Abraham, Isaac and Jacob and those who would reject it. Who among the children would be worthy of carrying on the critical task on hand? The story of Joseph and his brothers shows a family unit on the verge of unraveling. Will the family be capable of retaining their unity?

Jacob settles in the area where his father had lived in the land of Canaan. These are the chronicles of Jacob. The narrative shifts our attention to a seventeen year old lad, tending the sheep with his brothers, the sons of Bilhah and Zilpah, his father's wives. Overly earnest, Joseph brings his father a bad report about them.

Israel loves Joseph, the child of his old age, more than any of his other sons, spoiling him with a long colorful coat. His brothers seethe with jealousy, unable to say a peaceful word to him. The situation is worsened when Joseph relays a dream to them, seemingly justifying his superiority and upon hearing it, the brothers hate him all the more. "Listen to the dream I had," he says to them. "We were binding sheaves in the field, when my sheaf suddenly stood up erect. Your sheaves formed a circle around my sheaf, and bowed down do it." "Do you want to be our king?" retorted the brothers. "Do you intend to rule over us?" Joseph continues to share his dreams with his brothers, seemingly oblivious to the effect he is having on them. "I just had another dream," he tells his father and brothers. "The sun, the moon, and eleven stars, were bowing down to me." His father scolds him, saying, "What kind of dream did you have? Do you want me, your mother, and your brothers to come and prostrate ourselves on the ground to you?" Still his father suspends judgment (Genesis 37:1).

Jacob settled in the land where his father had lived, in all likelihood to continue his father and grandfather's work of outreach. As the eldest son of his beloved wife Rachel, Jacob favors Joseph, providing him with a long colorful tunic as a symbol of elevated status within the family. Joseph's older brothers, sons of different wives, resent this distinction. They see in a seemingly naïve Joseph a troubling sense of superiority and vanity. We are not privy to the nature of the "bad report" that Joseph reveals to his father concerning the brothers, though it clearly fuels their enmity and resentment. Further inciting the brothers are Joseph's fanciful dreams of grandeur. Does he really think he is superior to his brothers and that he will rule over them? It seems so from Joseph's recounting of his second dream. Not only do the sheaves of grain belonging to his brothers bow to Joseph's sheaf, but the very cosmos itself, sun, moon and stars pay homage to him!

In addition to natural sibling rivalry portrayed here, there is a lurking suspicion on the part of the brothers that Joseph seeks to usurp his brothers for the special legacy of their father. Is not their heritage to be shared amongst them all? Or would it be further divided between Jacob's children, as had been the case with both Abraham's and Isaac's sons? As much as Jacob remonstrates Joseph for his pride and naiveté, he senses something in Joseph's character that moves him to suspend his criticism.

Later Jacob asks Joseph to check on the welfare of his brothers who are out tending his sheep in Shechem, a request which Joseph obediently follows. In narrative laced with irony the Biblical text portends the ominous developments. Wandering around Shechem, Joseph meets a stranger who sees him blundering in the fields. " 'What are you looking for?' asks the stranger. 'I seek my brothers,' replied Joseph, 'perhaps you can tell me where they are tending the sheep' " (Genesis 37:15-16). The anonymous biblical stranger informs Joseph that his brothers have headed for Dothan.

The great medieval commentator Rashi, explains that this unnamed stranger is none other than the angel Gabriel. This comment on the biblical text points to the divine providential unfolding of events. Unsuspecting, Joseph innocently continues his search for his brothers and their welfare. Upon spotting him from afar, they conspire to kill him. The text shocks the reader in their apparent cruelty, the callous disregard displayed toward Joseph's life and the feelings of their elderly father Jacob.

> *"Here comes the dreamer!" they called to one another. "Now we have the chance! Let's kill him and throw him into one of the pits. We can say that a wild beast ate him. Then let's see what will become of his dreams!" Reuben heard these words and tried to rescue [Joseph]...Reuben tried to reason with his brothers. "Don't commit bloodshed. You can throw him into this well in the desert, and you won't have to lay a hand on him." His plan was to rescue [Joseph] from [his brothers] and bring him back to his father. When Joseph came to his brothers, they stripped him of the long colorful coat that he was wearing. They took him and threw him into the well. The well was empty; there was no water in it. The [brothers] sat down and ate a meal. When they looked up, they saw an Arab caravan coming from Gilead. The camels were carrying gum, balsam, and resin, transporting them to Egypt. Judah said to his brothers, "What will we gain if we kill our brother and cover his blood? Let's sell him to the Arabs and not harm him with our own hands. After all, he's our brother, our own flesh and blood." His brothers agreed. The strangers, who turned out to be Midianite traders approached, and [the brothers] pulled Joseph out of the well. They sold him to the Arabs for twenty pieces of silver. [These Midianite Arabs] were to bring Joseph to Egypt. When Reuben returned to the well, Joseph was no longer there. [Reuben] tore his clothes in grief. He returned to his brothers. "The boy is gone!" he exclaimed, "And I — where can I go?"*
>
> *[The brothers] took Joseph's coat. They slaughtered a goat and dipped the coat in the blood. They sent the long colorful coat, and it was brought to their father. "We found this," they said "Try to identify it. Is it your son's coat or not?"*

> *[Jacob immediately] recognized it. "It is my son's coat!" he cried. "A wild beast must have eaten him! My son Joseph has been torn to pieces!" He tore his robes in grief and put on sackcloth. He kept himself in mourning for many days. All his sons and daughters tried to console him, but he refused to be comforted. "I will go down to the grave mourning for my son," he said. He wept for [his son] as only a father could. The Midianites sold (Joseph) in Egypt to Potiphar, one of Pharaoh's officers, captain of the guard.*
>
> [Genesis 37:19-35]

Joseph, cruelly torn from his father and family, is sold into Egyptian servitude. His cloak of distinction, mark of his pride, becomes the symbol of his demise. However, Joseph prospers in his newfound surrounding. Joseph is one of a very select group of Biblical personalities described as having the gift of Divine "grace." This natural charisma, intelligence, and nobility, cannot be repressed despite his lowly status. He soon rises to enjoy unquestioned confidence of his master and becomes general manager of an Egyptian nobleman's household. All the affairs of the estate are in Joseph's hands. His attractiveness does not escape the eye of his master Potiphar's wife, who is unrelenting in her attempts to seduce Joseph. Joseph does not betray his master, nor does he dare to "sin before God" (Genesis 39:9). As a true son of Israel, Joseph could not tolerate this wanton immorality. Soon however, her manipulations increase in intensity. The woman grabs Joseph by his cloak, and pleads with him to sleep with her. Not trusting himself for a second, he flees, leaving the cloak in her hand. Feeling foolish and rejected, she screams, "He brought us a Hebrew man to play games with us! He came to rape me, but I screamed as loud as I could!" (Genesis 39:14-15). When Potiphar hears his wife's story, he becomes furious. Joseph's master has him arrested, and placed in the dungeon reserved for the king's prisoners. Joseph's plight worsens. Once again he is unjustly accused. Once again his cloak becomes the symbol of his undoing, reduced from slave to prisoner.

Yet the text informs us that again, "God was with Joseph," enabling him to rise up from the depths of the dungeon (Genesis 39:23). Soon the warden had placed all the prisoners in the dungeon under Joseph's charge, including the Pharaoh's chief steward and baker – fellow inmates of Joseph imprisoned by the king. Visiting them one morning, Joseph sees they are upset, and asks what is worrying them. Upon hearing of their troubling and perplexing dreams, Joseph relieves their anxiety by masterfully interpreting them. Each officer meets his fate exactly as predicted: the chief steward freed while the baker is hanged. Upon being freed from prison Joseph implores the steward to return the favor and mention his name to Pharaoh (Genesis 40:5-9, 14-16).

Here, Joseph errs. His urging the steward to intercede on his behalf mitigates the absolute wonder and awe that the steward had for Joseph and his prescient interpretation. Once the steward senses Joseph's dependence on him, Joseph's accomplishment is lessened. As a result, "the chief steward did not remember Joseph. He forgot all about him"(Genesis 40:23).[23]

Joseph languishes in prison for an additional two years until Pharaoh, absolute and deified ruler of Egypt, undergoes a foreboding nightmare. Traumatized, Pharaoh summons all his advisors and wise men; however none of them could satisfactorily explain the meaning of the dreams. At this point the chief steward remembers Joseph's interpretation and informs Pharaoh of what had transpired between them. Joseph is summoned, preened and pampered prior to his entrance before Pharaoh. Pharaoh says to Joseph, "I had a dream, and there is no one who can interpret it. I heard that when you hear a dream, you can explain it."

Joseph humbly shirks the compliment and attributes his prowess to G-d, assuring Pharaoh, "It is not by my own power. But God may provide an answer concerning Pharaoh's fortune." Pharaoh relates his dreams to Joseph:

> *"In my dream, I was standing on the bank of the Nile. Suddenly seven fat, handsome cows emerged from the Nile, and grazed in the marsh grass. Then, just as suddenly, seven other cows emerged after them, very*

> *badly formed and emaciated. I never saw such bad ones in all Egypt. The emaciated, bad cows proceeded to eat the first seven, healthy cows. These were completely swallowed by the [emaciated] cows, but there was no way of telling that they were inside. The cows looked just as bad as they had at first. Then I woke up. Then I had another dream. There were seven full, good ears of grain growing on one stalk. Suddenly, seven other ears of grain grew behind them. [The second ones] were shriveled, thin and scorched by the east [desert] wind. The thin ears swallowed up the seven good ears. I told this to the symbolists but none of them could interpret it for me."*
>
> [Genesis 41:17-25]

Joseph's perspicacious interpretation amazes Pharaoh. Joseph's distinction was in his interpreting the two dreams as different manifestations of a singular and imminent message; the seven thin cows, and the fat cows, the good ears of grain, and the bad ears of grain, as a singular allegory, foreshadowing seven years of famine overtaking seven years of plenty (Genesis 41:28-32).

Again, Joseph's proactive and charismatic personality comes to the forefront as he not only tersely and boldly explains Pharaoh's dream, but unabashedly gives unsolicited advice on governmental policy as well.

> *"Now Pharaoh must seek out a man with insight and wisdom, and place him in charge of Egypt. Pharaoh must then take further action, and appoint officials over the land. A rationing system will have to be set up over Egypt during the seven years of surplus. Let (the officials) collect all the food during these coming good years, and let them store the grain under Pharaoh's control. The food will be kept in cities under guard. The food can then be held in reserve for the land when the seven famine years come to Egypt. The land will then not be depopulated by the famine."*
>
> [Genesis 41:33-36]

Pharaoh and all his advisors are thoroughly impressed with the plan and with Joseph, declaring him a man of "God's spirit" and appointing him to a position of authority only second to himself. Joseph at age thirty, is not the same youth of seventeen whose tendency towards narcissism, obscured his natural leadership abilities. Thirteen years of suffering and degradation have transformed a prisoner into a prime minister. Joseph's natural brilliance, self confidence and talent are readily apparent to all, yet Joseph attributes his abilities solely to God. He is both a visionary and operations manager par excellence, and brings Pharaoh untold wealth while directing Egypt's natural resources. During the years of famine that ensue, the surrounding populations learn that there is sustenance in Egypt and all travel there for succor.

However, as history has shown time and time again, success bears the danger of assimilation. In naming his sons, Joseph articulates the double-edged quality of finding success in a society that is not one's own.

> *Joseph had two sons before the famine years came, borne by Asenath, daughter of Potiphar, priest of On. Joseph named the first born son Manasseh, "because God has made me forget all my troubles, and even my father's house." He named his second son Ephraim, "because God has made me fruitful in the land of my suffering."*
>
> [Genesis 41:50]

Has Joseph forgotten his family? Why did his father Jacob, a wealthy and capable man, not come looking for him? Has Joseph reconciled to the fact that he is permanently estranged from his family? What about the legacy of the family? Was Joseph excluded? As newly appointed Prime Minister Joseph certainly had the means to contact his father, why didn't he?

Joseph patiently waits for events to unfold. Despite his vast responsibilities as Prime Minister, Joseph personally oversees the food distribution to foreigners. The famine drives Jacob's family to hunger and Jacob's sons have no alternative but to travel to Egypt for provisions, placing them under Joseph's direct jurisdiction.

Joseph's ten brothers journey to buy grain in Egypt. Benjamin, as the youngest and "only" remaining son of Rachel, stays behind. When Joseph's brothers arrive, they prostrate themselves before him, faces to the ground. Though Joseph recognizes his brothers, he behaves like a stranger to them, seeing before him the prostrating sheaves and stars of his dreams, and recognizing the presence of the Divine hand in the orchestrating of this meeting. Not only does Joseph feign indifference, but antagonistically accuses them of being spies. Though the brothers plead their innocence, share their family history and invoke their father and brother back home, Joseph replies harshly, imprisoning them for three days, and demanding that they return with the youngest. The brothers share in their despair, and connect their current misfortune to the regrettable act of selling their brother. Joseph, who unbeknownst to them understands what they are saying, is so overcome with emotion that he is forced to leave the chamber. Joseph returns with a stern demeanor, taking Simon from them and placing him in chains before their very eyes (Genesis 42: 3-24).

Joseph, it seems, had in some sense anticipated his brothers' arrival in Egypt, and begins an elaborate ruse to put the brothers on the defensive and impugn their intentions. Laced with irony, the brothers, who did not recognize his cries for help many years prior, did not recognize him on that day either.

Joseph gives order to supply his brothers with grain and provisions for their journey, and places their money back into their sacks. When the brothers open up their packs in the midst of their travels, their hearts sink. "What is this that God has done to us?" they asked each other with trembling voices. Back home, they tell their father Jacob about all that had happened to them. Their father is inconsolable. "You're making me lose my children! Joseph is gone! Simon is gone, now you want to take Benjamin! Everything is happening to me!" (Genesis 42:25-33)

From his profoundly pained reaction, we see that Jacob had never recovered from the alleged "death" of Joseph, his beloved son. All these years he mourned and refused to be comforted. Now Jacob stood the risk of losing Benjamin, Joseph's younger brother, all that remained from his true love and primary wife Rachel.

Simon's abduction and the mysterious return of the brothers' money did not bode well for the family either.

Soon however, Jacob is again confronted with the decision of deciding his family's fate. The famine became worse in the area, and the supplies from Egypt had dwindled. Jacob wants to send his sons back for more provisions, but Judah reminds him of the ominous threat the Prime Minister had made them, "The man warned us, 'Do not appear before me unless your brother is with you.' " (Genesis 43:3). After extended questioning as to why the brothers revealed so much sensitive information, and hearing a stirring plea from Judah, who personally guarantees the safety of Benjamin, Israel finally consents to allow Benjamin to accompany them back to Egypt. He sends them off, laden with the choicest products of the land, and enough money to pay for the 'oversight' of the returned money. Before they leave, Israel parts with his children, not without a tinge of resigned desperation over the unfolding of events, "If I must lose my children, then I will lose them" (Genesis 43: 14).

Once again, the brothers stand before Joseph. When Joseph sees Benjamin with them, he summons the overseer of his household to bring the men into the palace and prepare a great feast. The brothers, thinking that they are being indicted for the money, begin professing their innocence to the overseer, who reassures them that the returned money must have been a gift from God. With that he brings out Simon to them (Genesis 43:15-23).

How flabbergasted the brothers must have been, to have suspected the worst and now were not only re-uniting with their brother Simon, but invited to be the honored guests at the palace of the Prime Minister himself. They presented him with the delicacies they had brought and answered inquiries to their father's welfare. Upon seeing Benjamin, Joseph again becomes overcome with emotion, prompting him to quickly leave the room and regain his composure (Genesis 43:25-3).

At the banquet the brothers are astounded that Benjamin is served five times as much as the rest of them receiving a seemingly undue measure of favoritism. While the brothers are sufficiently fed and intoxicated, Joseph has his overseer again return the money into the mens' sacks, also planting Joseph's silver divining chalice into Benjamin's bag as "evidence" to later accuse Benjamin of stealing. After leaving Egypt the brothers are pursued, and the missing chalice is discovered in Benjamin's sack. They are brought back to the palace, where the brothers stand before the Prime Minister, vehemently denying the claims to the point that they are willing to offer their lives as slaves. Joseph accepts the offer, but only to an extent, warning that only he in whose bag is found the chalice, will be kept as a slave. As the packs are opened one by one, the "truth" is uncovered, and the brothers tear their clothes in grief and prostrate themselves before Joseph. They offer themselves as slaves, but the "merciful" Joseph will only take Benjamin, leaving the rest to go in peace (Genesis 43:33-44:17).

The brothers are devastated. In this critical moment, the true test of their character is placed before them. How would the brothers react to Benjamin being accused of grand theft? Joseph's designs put the brothers in an untenable situation, very similar to one they faced many years before. Their brother Benjamin, with Joseph long gone, is now unquestionably Jacob's favorite. Forbidden to accompany the brothers to Egypt to secure provisions, it is only the incarceration of Simon, and the protracted famine, which forces Jacob to agree at last to send Benjamin and thus placate the Egyptian ruler's demands. Even so, Jacob was reluctant. Was not this good cause to arouse the brothers to be envious of Benjamin? After all Benjamin was safe at home with his father while the rest of the brothers undertook the hazardous journey to Egypt. Didn't this remind the brothers of Joseph who remained at home with his father when they had to tend the sheep!

A dramatic climax awaits the family of Jacob. The brothers, despondent, return to Egypt. Judah, the same brother who took charge in the operation to sell Joseph, appears again as leader, taking initiative and stepping forward in Benjamin's defense.

> *Judah walked up to [Joseph] and said, "Please your highness, let me say something to you personally. Do not be angry with me, even though you are just like Pharaoh. You asked if we still had a father or another*

brother. We told you, 'We have a father who is very old, and the youngest [brother] is a child of his old age. He had a brother who died, and thus, he is the only one of his mother's children still alive. His father loves him.' You said to us, 'Bring him to me, so that I may set my eyes on him.' We told you, 'The lad cannot leave his father. If he left him, his father would die.' You replied, 'If your youngest brother does not come with you, you shall not see my face again.' We went to your servant our father and told him what you said. When our father told us to go back and get some food, we replied, 'We cannot go. We can only go if our youngest brother is with us. If he is not with us we cannot even see the man [in charge].' Your servant our father said, 'You know that my wife [Rachel] bore me two sons. One has already left me, and I assume that he was torn to pieces by wild animals. I have seen nothing of him until now. Now you want to take this one from me too! If something would happen to him, you will have brought my white head down to the grave in evil misery.' And now, when I come to your servant our father, the lad will not be with us. His soul is bound up with [the lad's] soul! When he sees that the lad is not there, he will die! I will have brought your servant our father's white head down to the grave in misery. Besides, I offered myself to my father as a guarantee for the lad, and I said, 'If I do not bring him back to you, I will have sinned to my father for all time.'

'So now let me remain as your slave in place of the lad. Let the lad go back with his brothers! For how can I go back to my father if the lad is not with me? I cannot bear to see the evil misery that my father would suffer!' "

[Genesis 44:18-34]

The brothers have been placed in an untenable situation. Despite the evidence pointing to Benjamin's guilt, which could have easily justified leaving Benjamin to become a slave; despite the deeply harbored jealousy against Benjamin, who now was

Jacob's favored son; the brothers are contrite - they cannot leave Benjamin behind.

All the grief that Jacob endured at Joseph's loss and all the guilt that the brothers harbored for their actions coalesce at that moment. Judah could no longer bear to witness their father's sorrow. Judah comes to the defense of his brother, making a poignant plea appealing to the ruler's sensitivity and basic humanity, imploring him to exhibit kindness on behalf of his forlorn father. In a complete turnaround, Judah, the brother who devised the plan to sell their brother Joseph into slavery, now offers himself into slavery to protect a brother. Perhaps Judah perceives some compassion in the strange ruler who inquired of their family and father. Perhaps Judah harbored some suspicion as to the true identity of this Prime Minister who astonishingly seated each of the brothers in their correct birth order.

At this point Joseph understands that the brothers are sincerely remorseful, and have now redeemed themselves from their sin against him. In one of the most passionate passages of the Bible, Joseph finally reveals his true identity to his brothers.

> *Joseph could not hold in his emotions. Since all his attendants were present, he cried out, "Have everyone leave my presence!" Thus, no one else was with him when Joseph revealed himself to his brothers. He began to weep with such loud sobs that the Egyptians could hear. The news [of these strange happenings] reached Pharaoh's palace.*
>
> *Joseph said to his brothers, "I am Joseph! Is my father still alive?"*
>
> *His brothers were so startled, they could not respond. "Please come close to me," said Joseph to his brothers. When they came closer, he said, "I am Joseph your brother! You sold me to Egypt. Now don't worry or feel guilty because you sold me. Look! God has sent me ahead of you to save lives! There has been a famine in the area for two years, and for another five years there will be no plowing or harvest. God has sent me ahead of*

you to insure that you survive in the land and to keep you alive through such extraordinary means."

"Now it is not you who sent me here, but God. He has made me Pharaoh's vizier, director of his entire government, and dictator of all Egypt.

"Hurry, go back to my father, and give him the message — Your son Joseph says, 'God has made me master of all Egypt. Come to me without delay. You will be able to settle in the Goshen district and be close to me — you, your children, your grandchildren, your cattle, and all that you own. I will fully provide for you there, since there will still be another five years of famine. I do not want you to become destitute, along with your family and all that is yours. You and my brother Benjamin can see with your own eyes that I myself am speaking to you. Tell Father all about my high position in Egypt and about all that you saw. You must hurry and bring Father here."

[With that, Joseph] fell on the shoulders of his brother Benjamin, and he wept. Benjamin [also] wept on [Joseph's] shoulders. [Joseph] then kissed all his brothers and wept on their [shoulders].

[Genesis 45:1-13]

The family, torn asunder for so long, has reconciled. The hatred, jealousy, and enmity that lived amongst the brothers for so long, has now been assuaged.

Upon realizing that his son Joseph is indeed alive, Jacob's prophetic vision is renewed. God informs Jacob, now Israel, that he must leave Canaan, because it is only in Egypt that the family group will coalesce into a people (Genesis 46:1-7). Despite the fact that Jacob is reassured by God, and is certainly thrilled to reunite with his long-lost son Joseph, he is deeply disturbed by the fact that he must leave Canaan, the land promised to him and his descendants. He realizes that this was the beginning of a difficult prophetic tradition passed down from his grandfather Abraham; that the family will endure much suffering prior to their redemption from Egypt, condemned to be strangers in a land not their own.

The book of Genesis closes with a vision of Jacob's family's trek down to Egypt. The Bible recounts the full lineage of Jacob; each of his twelve sons and their respective families (Genesis 46:26-27). Not surprisingly, this extended family of souls, who would comprise the foundation of the children of Israel, is seventy in number. Tellingly, this number seventy, represents the same number of the descendants of Noah who formed the nucleus of the nations of the world (Genesis 10:1-31).

Here we see an astonishing parallel of Biblical intent. The seventy souls comprising the founding family of Israel parallel the seventy offspring of Noah, who form the primary nations of the world. It would become the task of the seventy descendants of Israel to begin the process of teaching the world community to reconcile and learn to live together in unity and harmony.

Unity of the whole is based on interdependence and reciprocity; this is one of the most critical lessons to be learned in these final chapters. Creating a community of educators and peacemakers would not be a quick or easy task, but would require a long period of gradual incremental steps — begun by Abraham, accepted by Isaac, and confirmed by Jacob. The nation they founded, Israel, is thus called precisely because it was Jacob who succeeded in having all of his children accept the challenge and task of beginning this process, for without familial unity there can be no national unity.

Jacob spends the final seventeen years of his life in Goshen, a private community in Egypt reserved for Jewish habitation. He is reunited with Joseph and the entire family is at peace. Jacob meets and blesses Pharaoh and the family enjoys their elevated status in the land. Prior to passing, Jacob gathers his twelve sons to give his final blessings.

A cursory reading of the blessings (Genesis 49:1-28) however, reveals quite a disparity in the blessing accorded to each son. The preferred blessings are accorded to both Judah and Joseph, while the words conferred upon Reuben, Simon, and Levi, on the other hand, seem not to be a blessing at all! Could it be that Jacob has not learned from the tragic consequences of favoring one child over another, a cause of untold suffering for the family? A careful reading of the final verse of the blessing discounts this possibility, as it is written, "All these are the tribes of Israel, twelve in all, and this is what their father said to them when he blessed *them.* He gave each one his own special blessing" (Genesis 49:28). In other words, Jacob blessed *all* his children, to enjoy the strengths and qualities that were most favorable to each individual. In that way the family would be blessed collectively. Each child would be blessed with the finest qualities of each of the rest of his siblings. Jacob dies and is taken to be buried back in the same Cave of the Patriarchs where Abraham and Sarah, Isaac and Rebecca, and his own wife Leah were buried.

Upon returning to Egypt however, the brothers begin to realize the implications of their father's death, fearing it will catalyze retribution from Joseph for all that they had done to him. They send messengers telling Joseph,

> *"Before he died, your father gave us final instructions. He said, 'This is what you must say to Joseph: Forgive the spiteful deed and the sin your brothers committed when they did evil to you.' Now forgive the spiteful deed that [we], the servants of your father's God, have done."*
>
> [Genesis 50: 16-17]

As he hears these words, Joseph weeps. Again he proclaims that he cannot judge them, for though they may have wished him harm, Divine providence had made things good; preserving him and his family, and enabling them to provide sustenance for the entire region at a critical time. The next we see of Joseph, the intimacy between the brothers seems to be fully restored, as Joseph entrusts the brothers with the task of interring his remains in the land of Israel:

> *Joseph remained in Egypt along with his father's family. He lived to be 110 years old. Joseph saw Ephraim's grandchildren, and the children of Manasseh's son Makhir were also born on Joseph's*

> *lap. Joseph said to his brothers, "I am dying. God is sure to grant you special providence and bring you out of this land, to the land that he swore to Abraham, Isaac, and Jacob." Joseph then bound the children of Israel [his brothers] by an oath: "When God grants you [this] special providence, you must bring my remains out of this place."*
>
> [Genesis 50:22-25]

In a brilliant analysis, Rabbi Joseph Soloveitchik posits that Joseph understood that the deep seated anxiety the brothers felt was due to Joseph's alleged superiority over them.[25] After all, his dreams of grandeur came true! Did they not all owe their (and their families') lives to Joseph as well? Joseph needed to finally and forcefully demonstrate to them that, in truth, they were truly interdependent: he needed his brothers as much as they needed him. Joseph places his trust in his brothers, bidding them, and not his sons, to eventually inter him in the land of Canaan. Only then could he assure his own ultimate burial in the land of Israel.

It is this lesson of mutual interdependence, what can be called a "proactive fellowship," that becomes the guiding principle for Jewish action throughout the ages. Each individual brother, with his distinctive and unique blend of personality and character, works together with the others to realize the goal of teaching the principles of ethical monotheism to the world. This paradigm of Joseph and his brothers, the twelve sons of Israel, acting in concert becomes the model for the Jewish people.

How noble a finale to the book of Genesis. We have seen that mankind in the paradigm of Adam and Eve, sin, as individuals against God. While they do so, each passes the blame, seeking to justify his or her own actions at another's expense. In our second paradigm we see individual man sinning against his fellow man. Tragedy ensues when even brothers, sharing the most natural and intimate of relationships, cannot accept each other. These failings are repeated on a grander scale, with men collectively sinning against their fellow men, culminating in the Deluge. Subsequently, in the narrative of the Tower of Babel, Man collectively sins against God, resulting in even more fragmentation, dispersion, and differentiation throughout the Earth.

Slowly, however, these repeated lapses begin to be corrected by Abraham, Isaac, Israel, and their children. Despite much suffering and anguish, a nucleus of a family is formed that is able to begin the slow, incremental work of redeeming humanity. With the close of the book of Genesis, we see a family reconciled, a nation soon-to-be born. What better an example to teach the rest of the family of nations about the ills and evils of slavery, oppression, and idolatry than a nation born through slavery, degradation and injustice? The book of Genesis is a book for all time. It is what my friend and mentor, Rabbi Shlomo Riskin, calls "eternally contemporary."

The Religious Personality

Human beings, reflective creatures that we are, are curious to make sense of our lives. Born to a specific place and time, to a family setting uniquely our own, the vast majority of us seek to understand our place in our family, community, and country, and as members of the human race. We come into the world through a specific set of circumstances and seek our own identity and place within the "grand scheme of things."

Why are we here? What are we to accomplish? What is life all about? How can we fulfill our goals? We experience pleasure and pain, frustration and fulfillment, invariably dealing with sorrow and success, happiness and helplessness, on so many levels. Though much has been written about how to achieve happiness and fulfillment in life, the most comprehensive and timely lessons are again to be found in the Hebrew Bible.

The Hebrew Bible, with its election of the children of Israel as God's chosen people, was to later become the mother of two great faiths: Christianity and Islam. However it must be stressed that the Jew's being "chosen" is not based on ethnicity, nor does it imply any notion of superiority. Rather, it means that Jews, and all members of the human family who wishes to embrace the principles and unique responsibilities of Jews, accept upon themselves a strict lifestyle dedicated to individual and collective improvement. The children of Israel strive towards perfection, or as close to it as is humanly achievable, by leading a purposeful life. This purposeful life is characterized by *mitzvoth*, Divine commandments which act as spiritual exercises, both mental and physical, and are designed to impart values and properly guide actions that pertain to even the most seemingly trite and mundane of human activity. We are reminded, through the performance of *mitzvoth*, every time we eat, drink, sleep, and perform bodily functions, to recognize the Creator and our role as his representatives. We are enjoined to lead a life of positive actions and purity, with ourselves and our fellow man. Much as an athlete adopts a rigorous diet and lifestyle as he trains for excellence in his chosen sport, the Jew adopts a rigorous diet and lifestyle to train for excellence in developing his spiritual personality, his character, and his moral wellbeing.

Christianity and Islam later to proclaimed that they supplanted the role of the Jewish people, and that they exclusively held the solution to directing Mankind to perfect itself. Both religions, both great faiths, have adherents who are genuinely convinced that their's is the legitimate and exclusive path to salvation.

September 11, 2001 abruptly changed the world. A simmering problem manifesting in dissatisfaction with and hatred of the West, modernity, and what may be loosely characterized as the Judeo-Christian tradition, exploded in the inferno of the Twin Towers. New York City and Washington DC, symbols of economic superiority and military dominance, were brutally assaulted, literally reduced to rubble. An enemy unconcerned with human life had dared to attack the world's superpower head-on.

Centuries of stagnant development, brutal oppression by despotic rulers, massive poverty and ignorance amidst a coterie of those possessing immense mineral wealth nurtured and coalesced into what has become a fundamentalist-militant form of Islam. This understanding of Islam posits that Islam can brook no compromise with unbelievers. *Allah*, God, is to be served by spreading the one true faith of Mohammad, throughout the world – even by the tip of the sword.

What, if any, common ground is there amongst Christians, Muslims, and Jews? Each tradition has a rich and varied heritage with a wide range of interpretations. Can they be reconciled? Can one tradition embrace the "good and decent" people of the other faith in a positive way? We will examine the nature of the religious personality as we attempt to answer these questions.

The pioneering American philosopher and psychologist William James wrote considerably about the role of religion in a person's life in his classic work T*he Varieties of Religious Experience*. There he marked many similarities in the nature of religious experience that span across different religions. For James, religion is "the feelings, acts, and experiences of individual men in their solitude, so far as they apprehend themselves to stand in relation to whatever they may consider to be the divine."[26] I would suggest that this "divinity," what most of us call God, goes beyond the abstract notion of the early Greek philosophers' idea of the "first cause." At the risk of oversimplification, I would say that most of us consider God to be not only the transcendent, impersonal God of creation, but also the intimate personal God who cares about us and what we do. This is the definition accepted by most monotheistic religions and depicted in the Hebrew Bible.

For James, religion and "Churches, once established, live at second-hand upon tradition; but the founders of every church owed their power originally to the fact of their direct personal communion with the divine. Not only the superhuman founders, the Christ, the Buddha, Mahomet (Mohammad), but all the originators of Christian sects have been in this case; so personal religion should still seem the primordial thing, even to those who continue to esteem it incomplete." According to James, every religion was spawned by its founder's initial intense religious experience, and the church followed after and explained how the founder perceived that his vision was to be realized.

The notable exception to the pattern of religions based upon a founder with a singular religious experience is Judaism. Despite the fact that Abraham realized the ethical imperative inherent in the belief in one Creator, it was only when the Jewish people at Sinai collectively experienced the awesome power of Revelation that the Jewish people were formed. Abraham, as we have shown, was the first to understand that not only was there a single God of Creation but that He also demanded of Man to lead his life in a certain way. In this sense he was the founder of the Jewish people. However it was only the collective experience at Sinai that makes the Jewish experience unique and binding on the Jew for all time. It is this Revelation to an entire nation that sets apart Judaism from all other faiths and religions. We are Jews not because the Lord revealed himself to Abraham but because he revealed himself to all the people of Israel.

Individuals of all faiths have had "religious experiences." In relation to what William James describes as "the reality of the unseen," suggests:

> *All our attitudes, moral, practical, or emotional as well as religious, are due to the "objects" of our consciousness, the things which we believe to exist, whether really or ideally, along with ourselves. Such objects may be present to our senses, or they may be present to only our thought. In either case they elicit from us a reaction; and the reaction due to things of thought is notoriously in many cases as strong as that due to sensible presences. It may even be stronger.*[27]

James work is a classic psychological analysis of the religious personality. He interviews hundreds of people, analyzing their perceptions and feelings on the subject of God. Here is but one of many quotations, showing the tangibly strong presence of God in the life of a believer:

> *God is more real to me than any thought or thing or person. I feel his presence positively, and the more as I live in closer harmony with his laws as written in my body and mind. I feel him in the sunshine or rain; and awe mingled with a delicious restfulness most nearly describes my feeling. I talk to him as a companion in prayer and praise, and our communion is delightful. He answers me again and again, often in words so clearly spoken that it seems my outer ear must have carried the tone, but generally in strong mental impressions. Usually a text of Scripture, unfolding some new view of him and his love for me, and care for my safety. I could give hundreds of instances, in school matters, social problems, financial difficulties, etc. That he is mine and I am his never leaves me, it is an abiding joy. Without it life would be a desert, a shoreless, trackless waste.*[28]

Though many may discount the existence of God, even the skeptic and arch-rationalist cannot deny that so many people are affected by the "reality of the unseen." As James explains, "revelations of a kind of reality which no adverse argument, however unanswerable by you in words, can expel from your belief." This sort of experience James deems to be mystical, as opposed to "rational," which he defines according to four basic criteria. The rational experience requires, according to James, "definite statable abstract principles; definite facts of sensation; definite hypothesis based on such facts; and definite inferences logically drawn."[29]

James recognizes the classic dichotomies in the human personality: rational vs. emotional, sensory vs. intuitive. While acknowledging the rational, James also explores the depth of the religious mind in the non- and meta-rational aspects of the human personality. James sees both positive and negative manifestations of this non-rational aspect of the human personality, identifying two main religious personality types. The first, who reap the positive effects of religious thinking, follow what James deems the "religion of the healthy minded." This mindset is displayed by those whose chief concern in life is gaining, keeping, and restoring happiness. These people have an optimistic, cheerful nature, always looking to "get along" and "make do." To James, this life-affirming attitude is not only constructive, but widespread even amongst segments of the population who may not consider themselves "religious" under the traditional definition of the word. He explains that

> *[...] healthy mindedness as a religious attitude is therefore consistent with important currents in human nature and is anything but absurd. In fact we do all cultivate it more or less, even when our professed theology should in constancy forbid it. We divert our attention from disease and death as much as we can; and the slaughter houses and indecencies without end on which our life is founded are huddled out of sight and never mentioned, so that the world we recognize officially in literature and in society is a poetic fiction far handsomer and clear and better than the world that really is.*[30]

On the other end of the scale of the religious personality lies what James calls the "sick soul." Melancholy, brooding, and an obsession with death and evil, mark this religious orientation. Guilt, whether due to the inescapability of the "Original Sin," or sinful ways and habits in general, constantly gnaw at this personality. This personality type is at times plagued by what James characterizes as "demons of the mind."[31]

There exist also variations and combinations of these religious personalities, whom James characterizes as those with a "divided self." Some people vacillate between extremes of melancholy and dread on one hand, and happiness and contentment on the other. Often, these people undergo what is described as "rebirth," such as is common amongst those who consider themselves "born again Christians" in the Christian evangelical community.

Continuing up the spiritual ladder of religious personalities is what James describes as "saintliness." He quotes Dr. W.R Inge, to describe these personalities as people who claim to have an "immediate experience" with God, seeing his "footprints everywhere in nature, and feel his presence within them as the very life of their life," avoiding any action that distances one from God, the ways of "darkness and death," namely "self-seeking," and "sensuality in all its forms."[32]

According to James, the individual reaching saintliness displays characteristics of asceticism in shunning pleasures of the flesh as an expression of loyalty to a higher power; strength of the soul, exhibiting no anxiety or inhibitions, and purified from the brutal and sensual elements of the world. James was not so naïve however as to discount the often deleterious aspects of the saintly personality's religious experience. Extravagance, fanaticism, delusion, morbidity, and dementia were often the outcome of this personality's passionate cleaving unto his god. It is equally important to point out that James was a believing Christian and although most of the descriptions of a religious personality's experiences crossover into different religions, some are often not equivalent or experienced to the same degree.

One of the most profound and powerful of religious experiences is the mystical experience. This experience, though eschewing characterization by its nature, generally conforms to what James identifies as four aspects. A person will usually find his experience impossible to define; ineffable, or indescribable, needing of experience to be truly appreciated. The mystical incident will also have a noetic quality, imparting some sort of knowledge or illumination. Finally, experiences of the mystical sort are usually both transient and passive, occurring beyond their control and fleeting before a full meaning of the experience could be grasped.[33]

George Fox, a founder of the Christian Protestant Quaker sect, describes his mystical experience in his Journal. There he writes:

> *I fasted much, walked about in solitary places many days, and often took my Bible, and sat in hollow trees and lonesome places until night came on; and frequently in the night walked about by myself, for I was a man of sorrows in the time of the first workings of the Lord in me.*
>
> *During all this time I was never joined in profession of religion with any, but gave up myself to the Lord, having forsaken all evil company, taking leave of father and mother, and all other relations, and traveling up and down as a stranger on the earth, which way the Lord inclined my heart; taking a chamber to myself in the town where I came, and tarrying sometimes more, sometimes less, in a place […] As I had forsaken the priests, so I left the separate preachers also, and those called the most experienced people; for I saw there was none among them all that could speak to my condition […] I heard a voice which said, "There is one, even Jesus Christ, that can speak to thy condition." When I heard it, my heart did leap for joy. Then the Lord let me see why there was none upon the earth that could speak to my condition […] I was afraid of all carnal talk and talkers, for I could see nothing but corruptions. When I was in the deep, under all shut up, I could not believe that I should ever overcome; my troubles, my sorrows,*

> *and my temptations were so great that I often thought I should have despaired, I was so tempted. But when Christ opened to me how he was tempted by the same devil, and had overcome him, and had bruised his head; and that through him and his power, life, grace, and spirit, I should overcome also, I had confidence in him. If I had had a king's diet, palace, and attendance, all would have been as nothing for nothing gave me comfort but the Lord by his power.* (*Journal*, 59-61)

These writings, no doubt penned by a sensitive soul, demonstrate an interesting irony. When writings such as these, by Fox, or a kindred spirit, imposed a new doctrine adopted by others of the time, this new doctrine was initially deemed a heresy by other sects. However, after adoption and acceptance by others, the new doctrine itself became orthodoxy. What of the spiritual ruminations or mystical experiences of those who espouse a new doctrine? Are these the callings of the perceptive soul, the delusions of a madman, or pleas of a prophet? There seems to be no way of knowing.

Unless a person is a complete charlatan, there is no reason to doubt the veracity of the saint, the born-again, or the mystic's experience — for the one experiencing these phenomena. However, the question is not whether that individual had a truthful or overwhelming religious experience but what message or lesson can be derived from that experience. Does he adopt for himself, or ask of others to adopt, a specific set of rules, actions, or beliefs? Does he have specific knowledge that he feels compelled to impart to others?

The standard by which to evaluate any and every individual religious experience is contained in the Hebrew Bible, and it is the Seven Noahide principles for the gentile and the 613 precepts for the Jew.

Though James's study is quite comprehensive, he does not go into any detail about the nature of the most profound of religious experiences: prophecy. No doubt this is due to the fact that prophecy, in the Biblical sense, is no longer active. Jewish tradition dates the end of prophecy to the destruction of the First Temple (586 BCE), when prophetic communication was silenced, only to be reintroduced in the Messianic Era. Let us explore the nature of the Hebrew Bible's understanding of prophecy and the collective prophetic experience at Sinai.

The Prophetic Experience

That prophecy exists is an indication that the Creator is caring and benevolent. Unlike the doctrine of Deism, which holds that the creator and the universe are one (implying an impersonal and uncaring god), the phenomena of prophecy demonstrates that God the Creator wants to communicate, impart knowledge and enlightenment to his created. He has not left man bereft of guidance and direction The proof of this is that he has revealed himself, through the prophetic encounter, to the selected few throughout history.

Prophecy is the most profound, awesome, and powerful of religious experiences, overwhelming, and indescribable, permanently altering the consciousness of the one experiencing it. Prophecy was not only emotionally taxing but physically debilitating as well. Daniel describes his prophetic ordeal as a whole body experience, in which "joints shuddered and I could retain no strength, how can this servant of my Lord speak with this my lord? From now on no strength will remain in me, and there is no breath left in me!" (Daniel 10:15)

Moses Maimonides, the medieval giant of Jewish law and thought, thoroughly explores this amazing phenomena in his *Fundamental Principles of the Torah.* There he writes:

> *It is one of the basic principles of religion that God inspires men with the prophetic gift. But the spirit of prophecy only rests upon the wise man who is distinguished by great wisdom and strong moral character, whose passions never overcome him in anything whatsoever, but who by his rational faculty always has his passions under control, and possesses a broad and sedate mind. When one, abundantly endowed with these qualities and physically sound, enters the "Paradise" [prophetic encounter] [....] and continually dwells upon those great and abstruse themes, having the*

> *right mind capable of comprehending and grasping them; sanctifying himself, withdrawing from the ways of the ordinary run of men who walk in the obscurities of the times, zealously training himself not to have a single thought of the vanities of the age and its intrigues, but keeping his mind disengaged, concentrated on higher things… On such a man the Holy Spirit will promptly descend [...] He will be changed into another man and will realize that he is not the same as he had been, and has been exalted above other wise men, even as it is said of Saul, "And thou shalt prophesy with them, and shalt be turned into another man" (Samuel I:10:6).*[35]

For Maimonides, the classic expositor of Jewish tradition, the individual suited for prophecy had to have achieved the perfections of moral character, physical fitness, and intellectual accomplishment, in order to be blessed with an additional component of Divine grace.[36]

To Maimonides there are two forms of prophecy in the Hebrew Bible: the prophecy of Moses, and those of all the other prophets. Moses' level of prophecy was of a higher level than all others, communicated directly, rather than through veiled message. This is corroborated when God admonishes Miriam and Aaron, sister and brother of Moses, prophets in their own right.

> *[God] said, "Listen carefully to my words. If someone among you experiences divine prophecy, then when I make Myself known to him in a vision, I will speak to him in a dream. This is not true of my servant Moses, who is like a trusted servant throughout my house. With him I speak face to face, in a vision not containing allegory, so that he sees a true picture of God."*
>
> [Numbers 12:6-8]

In his classic *Guide of the Perplexed,* Maimonides further distinguishes between the prophecy of Moses vis-a-vis the other prophets. Moses would perform his signs and wonders in the presence of the antagonistic Egyptians eager to deride him and the entire nation who was positively disposed toward him. Later prophets however, had few or no witnesses to corroborate their story.[37]

Notwithstanding the unique character of Moses' prophecy as described in the Guide for the Perplexed, the binding authority of the law for Israel is not based even on the singular prophetic level of Moses, but rather on the collective revelation: the prophetic experience of the entire people of Israel at Sinai. In his *Fundamental Principles of the Torah*, Maimonides elaborates on this important principle:

> *Israel did not believe in Moses, our Teacher, on account of the wonders he showed. For when one's faith is founded on tokens, a lurking doubt always remains in the mind that these tokens may have been performed with the aid of occult arts and witchcraft. After all, the signs Moses showed in the wilderness he performed because they were needed, and not to support his prophetic claims[...] What were the grounds for faith in him? The Revelation on Sinai which we saw with our own eyes, and heard with our own ears, not having to depend on the testimony of others, we ourselves witnessed the fire, the thunder, the lightning, Moses entering the thick darkness after which the Divine Voice spoke to him, while we heard the call, "Moses, Moses, go tell them thus and thus" [...] Whence do we know that the Sinaitic revelation is the sole proof that Moses' prophecy is true? From the text, "Lo I come to speak unto thee in a thick cloud, that the people may hear when I speak unto thee, and may also believe in thee forever" (Exodus 19:9).*[38]

The Revelation at Sinai was the only incident of mass collective prophecy in the history of human experience, recorded at the very time it occurred. Each individual perceived the experience based on their own spiritual standing. Each man, woman and child apprehended an overwhelming experience that solidified the Jewish people into a "kingdom of priests and a holy nation"(Exodus 19:6). This "collective national memory" made the Law of Israel binding for all time upon the nation of Israel.[39]

It is against this backdrop of the *sui generis* experience of the Jewish people at Sinai that we must view all subsequent prophetic accounts.

What then of the "prophecies" of Jesus and Mohammad, founders of Christianity and Islam? Jesus and Mohammad did not have any collective prophetic experiences with their followers, nor do they have masses of people who witnessed and recorded these miracles when they occurred. Jesus and Mohammad may certainly have had profound religious experiences. They certainly had followers who acclaimed them as leaders and adapted their experiences and teachings. However from the Jewish standpoint, their experiences do not validate the changes in action or belief that they ask of their followers, nor do they rival the authority of the Sinai revelation.

Despite Judaism's unique Sinaitic experience, from the Jewish perspective all those who observe the Noahide precepts in the blessings of eternal life, no matter their faith. Christianity and Islam exclude from salvation all who do not accept the belief in Jesus or Mohammad. According to these faiths, even a righteous life of kindness and good deeds could not spare a non-believer in Jesus or Mohammad eternal damnation and suffering. How could a benevolent caring God, grant salvation to an evil person just for professing a belief in a particular individual, and at the same time damn a perfectly righteous individual who does not accept this message?

Family Politics

We have proposed that the Hebrew Bible is God's universal message to mankind, guiding humanity in how to lead a purposeful and ethical life. For the gentile, that means adopting the Noahide Laws, and for the Jew, the rigorous code of 613 Biblical precepts (and many more rabbinic enactments). These commandments apply to the Jew individually and to the Jewish people collectively. As a people, the Jewish nation's mission is to establish a just society in the land promised to the Patriarchs, designed to serve as an example for the family of nations.

With the destruction of the Second Jewish Temple in Jerusalem in the year 70 C.E., and the dissolution of the Jew's national sovereignty in Israel at the hands of the Roman empire, the Jewish people entered into millennia of exile and dispersion. Any notions concerning the collective national mission of Israel were relegated to hopeful prayers and distant dreams. The Jew's acceptance by society was by no means assured or taken for granted. The Jew was an apostate, an infidel doomed to suffer because of his rejection of Jesus, and later Mohammad. Little attention could be given to the Jewish national mission of universal redemption when Jews were persecuted in the many lands of their exile. A minimalist approach was adopted, whereby the Jew sought what was at best religious autonomy to the greatest degree possible for himself and his immediate community. This expressed itself by the Jew trying to practice his rituals and traditions as much as would be tolerated by his host country.

The condition of the Jew from the period of the destruction of the Temple in late antiquity throughout the Middle Ages was that of a sojourner, under constant threat of persecution, oppression, discrimination, and expulsion. Although select Jewish communities may have prospered and even flourished at particular points in time, most of this long span of approximately 2000 years was characterized by bitter hardship, persecution, and degradation.

The period of the Enlightenment, ushered in modern times and spawned the development of democracy, the notion of human rights, and the modern nation-state. Nevertheless this did not prevent the Second World War and the Holocaust, arguably the nadir of cruelty throughout human history.

An intelligent case may be made for the notion that the by-products of the age of Enlightenment led to the extreme positions that justified the excesses and evils of fascism and communism. In the case of communism, the seemingly positive idea that all citizens would share in the equal distribution of capital and wealth, led to a Stalin, who could kill tens of millions in order to purge society of any vestige of individualism and private enterprise. The idea of fascism, born from the differentiation and exaltation of certain races was embodied in the new nation-states, leading to a Hitler, whose Aryan nation was to lead humanity and rid the world of the lowly nation of Jews.

With the brutal assault on the United States on September 11, 2001, the world entered a new era. Samuel Huntington noted sociologist, famously characterizes this new era as "a clash of civilizations and the remaking of the world order." In his noted book of the same name, he proposes that the two hundred or so current independent nations of the world may be grouped roughly into eight major civilizations. These civilizations transcend a country's specific boundaries and are defined by and encompass what are roughly similar social, religious, historical, geographical, and linguistic features. Our family of man, dispersed into what Genesis described as 70 primary nations, can also be grouped amongst Huntington's delineations: Western, African, Sinic, Hindu, Islamic, Japanese, Latin-American, and Orthodox (Russian and Eastern European) civilizations.

The West, representing mainly the United States and Western Europe has dominated the globe politically, economically, militarily, and technologically, for the past 400 years. The West reached the zenith of its power and influence approximately at the time of the First World War. Now however, relative to other civilizations in the world, the West is in a steady, slow, and inexorable decline. With the power and influence shifting amongst civilizations, what is to be the future of the family of man? Will the family be better able to get along or will we be subject to a more volatile and unstable world order?

With the spectacular advances made in recent decades, specifically in the fields of communications, military, and biological technology, we have come across a paradoxical scenario. Despite the burgeoning world population and increased sophistication of organizations and government, the individual can affect and influence the masses on a scale never before imagined. We can only imagine the danger and havoc a lone or small group of terrorists in possession of certain weapons of mass destruction could wreak upon the world. On the other hand, consider the salutary benefits an inspired individual could affect, using mass communication to reach out to the world's masses with the proper message of hope and reconciliation.

Is there room for mutual acceptance among believers in the Hebrew Bible? Is there such a thing as an Abrahamic faith that brings together the Christian, Moslem and Jew? How does the rest of humanity fit in this scenario? Never before has the message of the Hebrew Bible, with its particularistic code for Jews, and its universal message through the Noahide precepts, been so much in need of being disseminated and actualized.

Nowhere is a civilization's or religion's goals and hopes so reflective of its values than in its eschatology, its vision of the "end of days." For the individual, this includes thoughts about life after death. For humanity as a whole, this covers the goals and presumed last stages of human development. Neither Christianity, Islam, nor Judaism has views of the end of days that are entirely monolithic. All have richly developed notions concerning their respective holy texts, creeds, and essential beliefs.

Christianity teaches that at the "end of days" a resurrected Jesus will return as *Christos*, Greek for messiah. This messiah is not human, but rather believed to be "son of God" in a literal sense; both fully human and simultaneously divine. Christian theology teaches that through his self sacrifice, Jesus offers salvation to all. The liberation and peace brought about by the messiah in

Christian thought is primarily a spiritual peace and liberation. Any political liberation is not considered to be an issue at all or at best is secondary. All an individual needs to do to be "saved" and not "damned" is to believe in Jesus as the savior of the world. Although much of Christianity teaches that God also wants people to do good deeds, good works alone will not lead to salvation.

Saint Paul, or Saul of Tarsus, was the individual most responsible for developing Christian theology. He taught that the "law" was abolished. No longer was it necessary to obey the legal strictures of what he termed the "Old Testament" since "we are in him and he is in us; he has died for all; he has crucified in himself our flesh of sin; by dying on the cross he has fulfilled for us the whole Law. Our flesh is considered as dead if Christ is in us. He who is dead is freed from sin"(Romans 6:7).

Time and again the Catholic Church and subsequent major Protestant denominations have restated this doctrine that faith alone is all that is necessary for a person to achieve eternal salvation. As Christianity developed, one would have thought that the issue of the importance of good works would have gained ascendancy. Nevertheless, 15th Century Church reformer John Huss teaches the same doctrine. Martin Luther later pronounces good works "mortal sins." John Calvin, with no connection to Luther or the Catholic Church proclaims, "we believe that by faith alone we share the righteousness of Jesus Christ. God had no regards for good works."[42] Even the Anglicans, considered to be one the more moderate of denominations announced in 1562 that, "good works, the products of faith even, cannot expiate our sins and satisfy the strict justice of God [...] As to those done without the grace of Jesus, they are but mortal sins."[43]

Some Christian denominations attempt to mitigate the insistence on blind faith alone as the road to salvation by requiring "transformational faith in Jesus," which expresses itself in good works as a "testament" to one's faith for others to see.

In March 2006, the Jerusalem Post published a piece on the evangelical pastor John Hague, and prominent Christian leader Reverend Jerry Falwell, and their espousal of an innovative

Christian belief referred to as the "dual covenant." This creed, running counter to mainstream Evangelical Christian thought, proposes that the Jewish people have a special relationship to God through the revelation at Sinai, and therefore do not need to "go through Christ or the Cross" to get to heaven. Unfortunately, a few days later, the newspaper printed another article whereby Hagee and Falwell repudiated these bold ideas.[44]

Apparently the backlash in the Christian community had forced these thinkers to rescind these bold new understandings. The notion of the importance of ethical and proper actions, as well as the admissibility of non- Christians into the "kingdom of heaven" would have represented a positive step in Christianity's development from the point of view of Judaism, one that brings it closer to its "parent."

Islam also fosters an elaborate tradition concerning the end of days. For Moslems the *Mahdi* is the messiah or savior. In his *Islamic Messianism*, Abdulaziz Sachedina describes the *Mahdi* as the leader prophesied to launch a great social transformation and bring *Allah*, God, to the world, while simultaneously restoring the purity of the faith in the prophet Mohammad as the final and greatest prophet. Islamic temporal rule will follow bringing Islamic governance to all the family of nations. The *Mahdi* will be a descendant of Mohammad as well as carry his name. He will emerge as an unrivalled political, military, and spiritual leader that will lead a revolution designed to establish a new world order. In his military campaign and "holy war," he will conquer Israel for Islam and establish world headquarters in Jerusalem. The faithful Moslems will battle and slaughter the remaining infidels, Jews and Christians. According to most Islamic scholars, Islam will emerge as the world's only religion.[45]

It is not the purpose of this work to fully explore the nature of Christianity's or Islam's visions of the future, nor their understanding of what we may call the "end of days" as it pertains to the culmination of our current view of human history, or "life after death" on an individual level. Indeed there is variance within the Christian, Islamic, and Jewish tradition as to how this will occur. What is important to our study is who will be eligible to enjoy the benefits of the blessings at the end of days and afterlife? According to mainstream Christian and Islamic thought, blessings accrue to the "believers" and conversely the curses apply to infidels, non believers in Jesus or Mohammad.

Judaism, and Noahism, as we shall see, are radically different in this regard.

Righteous Gentile or Convert?

From our study so far, we have learned that the Noahide, the righteous gentile who observes the Seven Principles, is also judged to be an individual that is deserving in God's eyes. The Talmud concludes that the righteous gentile (i.e., the Noahide) has a share in the world to come, as does the righteous Jew.[46]

However, what is preferable? Is the Noahide, who carefully observes the universal principles of right and moral living, equal in stature to the Jew, who is born into a complex and demanding set of rules and regulations? Or is the Jew, subject to myriad daily spiritual and legal exercises, on a higher spiritual plane than the less demanding claims made of the righteous gentile? Does God prefer Jews to Noahides?

The solution to this question lies in understanding the Biblical personality of Jethro. Jethro, Moses' father-in-law and a righteous gentile, is no ordinary figure. We first learn of him when Moses, who had grown up as a prince in the Pharaoh's household, flees to Midian from Egypt. Moses, the first recorded social activist, leaves the cushy royal palace to see the "suffering of his brethren." Upon seeing an Egyptian taskmaster beating a helpless Jewish slave, Moses smites the Egyptian officer, killing him. Upon being discovered as a defender of the Jews, Moses flees Pharaoh's wrath and escapes to Midian, where we find him at the local well, interceding on behalf of the daughters of the local sheik who were being harassed by the town's shepherds. Upon hearing his daughter's account of a stranger's brave intervention, Jethro invites Moses for dinner. and their relationship quickly blossoms.

Jethro, also known as *Reuel*, (Hebrew "friend of God") as well as several other names, was no ordinary Midianite, but a *cohen,* priest, of Midian. The classic commentaries explain that Jethro was a disillusioned priest who had apparently abandoned paganism. This change of beliefs made Jethro's daughters unpopular, treated cruelly by their fellow shepherds and forced to return home only after the other shepherds had already watered their own flocks. Only because of Moses' intercession on their behalf were the daughters able to water the flocks and return home early.

Jethro's sense of decency is also reflected in his chastisement of his daughters for seemingly abandoning the stranger who had come to their aid. Moses, impressed with his host and family, stays to live with Jethro and marries Tzipporah, Jethro's daughter. According to tradition, Moses lives with his father-in-law tending sheep for a period of forty years.

Moses is initiated into prophecy at the age of eighty, at the dramatic encounter at the "burning bush." However reluctant at first, Moses is cajoled by The Lord into assuming the momentous task of returning to Egypt to liberate his people from servitude. Returning to his father-in-law, Moses, gripped by the spirit of prophecy asks permission to "return to my people in Egypt to see if they are still alive." "Go in peace" is Jethro's reply (Exodus 4:18).

Moses returns to Egypt and together with his brother Aaron, challenges Pharaoh. In the fascinating biblical narrative that follows, a clash of civilizations ensues. Moses announces, "You must say to Pharaoh, this is what God says: Israel is My son, My firstborn. I have told you to let my son go and serve Me" (Exodus 4:22-23).

Egypt, known as the "empire of the first born," the world's superpower, is rudely challenged by Moses, the former prince espousing loyalty to a strange Being, with ideas of monotheism, free-will, life and liberty. To a culture whose crowning attributes were paganism, superstition, death worship, and servitude, Moses' pronouncements were shocking. Subsequently we learn of the dramatic episodes of the punishment of Egypt through the ten plagues and the miraculous exodus from Egypt by the people of Israel. The splitting of the sea brings final Divine retribution meted out to Pharaoh, his mighty cavalry and legions drowned by the very same waters that snuffed the life of the male Israelite infants cruelly drowned by the Egyptians.

In an underappreciated and seemingly unassuming section of the biblical narrative, Jethro returns to the scene. Having heard of all that God had done for the Jews in their Exodus from Egypt, Jethro leaves Midian and meets up with the Jewish people:

> *Jethro came together with Moses' wife and sons to the desert, where Moses was staying, near God's mountain.... Moses went out to greet his father-in-law, bowing down low and kissing him. They asked about each other's welfare and went into the tent. Moses told his father-in-law about all that God had done to Pharaoh and Egypt for the sake of Israel, as well as all the frustrations they had encountered on the way, and how God had rescued them. Jethro expressed joy because of all the good that God had done for Israel, rescuing them from Egypt's power. He said, "Praised be God, who rescued you from the power of Egypt and Pharaoh, who liberated the people from Egypt's' power. Now I know that God is the greatest of all deities. Through their very plots, He rose above them." Jethro brought burnt offerings and sacrifices to God. Aaron and all the elders of Israel came to share the meal with Moses' father-in-law before God.*
>
> *The next day, Moses sat to judge the people. They stood around Moses from morning to evening. When Moses' father-in-law saw all that [Moses] was doing for the people, he said, "Why are you sitting by yourself and letting all the people stand around you from the morning until evening? [...] You are going to wear yourself out, along with this nation that is with you. Your responsibility is too great. You cannot do it all alone. Now listen to me. I will give you advice, and God will be with you. You must be God's representative for the people, and bring their concerns to God. Clarify the decrees and laws for the people. Show them the path they must take, and the things they must do. But you must also seek out from among all the people capable, God-fearing men, men of truth, who hate injustice. You must then appoint them over (the people) as leaders of thousands, leaders of hundreds, leaders of fifties, and*

> *leaders of tens. Let them administer justice for the people on a regular basis. Of course, they will have to bring every major case to you, but they can judge the minor cases by themselves...." Moses took his father-in-law's advice, and did all that he said.*
>
> [Exodus 18:1-27]

Jethro is the archetypal righteous gentile. He rejoices in God's redemption of the children of Israel and notes the irony in Egypt's defeat. He counsels Moses in the single positive precept that he as a Noahide is responsible to observe: that of establishing the proper judicial instruments to equitably govern society. Moses, whose recent assumption of leadership demands the proper executive and judicial organization is advised to select God fearing people "men of truth, who hate injustice." This positive precept, universally critical to the proper functioning of a just society, is later greatly expanded upon in Jewish law, providing the bedrock for executing Gods Sinaitic revelation.

Jethro's council is so crucial that it intentionally precedes the most significant event to occur in human history: the Revelation of the Decalogue at Sinai, whereby the Jewish nation ratifies their constitution and pledges themselves to God and His law. Jethro's own drive to God's message, so readily ignored by the other nations, provides an inspiring prelude to the Jewish people's mass acceptance of God's will.

Jethro appears in the text again, this time in the book of Numbers, almost a full year after the Revelation at Sinai. The setting is profound. The people had just completed construction of the *Mishkan*, or Tabernacle, a portable "mini-temple" to accompany them on their journey into the Promised Land. The biblical text continues to describe a very elaborate census, and a detailed description of the physical layout of the Camp of Israel in the desert, followed by a seemingly tedious and repetitive description of the census and finally the inaugural ceremony of the Tabernacle in the midst of the camp. This Tabernacle held the Holy Ark which housed the stone tablets, "Tablets of Testimony" that Moses brought down from Sinai. The Holy Ark in which the

Tablets were ensconced also becomes the focal point for all subsequent prophetic encounters. Encounters between the Lord and Moses, beheld and attested to by the entire Children of Israel, were to continue in the Holy of Holies, the inner sanctum of the Tabernacle that housed the Ark. Throughout the sojourn in the desert, Moses continued to confront the Divine voice through meditation at, or on, the Holy of Holies (Numbers 7:8-9)

The camp, with the Tabernacle in its midst, was to travel with the people as they conquered the promised land and established the ideal society envisioned by the Patriarchs and promised by God to Abraham, Isaac, and Jacob, and reiterated at Sinai.

Each of the twelve tribes has a place and a flag in the camp, with three tribes each to the north, south, east and west of the Tabernacle, and a prince leading the way. Everything is readied for action, when the text abruptly turns to Jethro:

> *Moses said to his father-in-law "We are now on our way to the place that God promised to give us. Come with us and we will let you share the benefit of all the good things that God has promised Israel." "I would rather not go," replied [Jethro]. I wish to return to my land and my birthplace." "Do not abandon us," said Moses. "After all, you are familiar with the places where we are going to camp in the desert and you can be our guide. If you go with us, we will share with you whatever good God grants us."*
>
> [Numbers 10:28-32]

Jethro feels isolated. After witnessing the elaborate organization of the camp, with each and every member of the children of Israel given a specific name, place of belonging and purpose, Jethro feels he does not belong, that he has no place in the divine camp—or divine mission. Moses astutely senses his father-in-law's discomfort and magnanimously offers a share of the blessing awaiting Israel when they conquer and settle the Promised Land. The Biblical text however is deafeningly silent about Jethro's response.

Why? What does Jethro decide? Does he accompany Moses and the Children of Israel into the land as an adopted member of the people? Or does he return to Midian land of his birthplace? The very fact that the biblical narrative does not tell us of Jethro's decision speaks loudly about God's attitude towards our question. The answer is profound and sublime; for the Gentile there is no preference to being a Noahide, a righteous citizen of the world, or to choosing to convert to Judaism. God, the Creator and Sustainer, does not have a preference to the Jew over the Noahide. All that he asks is that we fulfill the directive that we are given. For the Gentile that is to be a Noahide, faithfully observing the Seven Principles of universal morality. For the Jew it is to realize a special selective calling that imposes extra responsibilities and obligations and to set an example that is to be emulated by the remainder of humanity. However noble a calling, the Noahide is not asked or required to assume it. That is precisely why Judaism has never actively sought out converts.

Judaism does however *accept* converts. Indeed many of the greatest personalities in Jewish history have been converts or children of converts. An amazing example of this attitude is found in the Babylonian Talmud:

> *Our rabbi's taught: It happened with a high priest that as he came forth from the Sanctuary [praying on behalf of the Jewish people on the Day of Atonement, holiest day of the Jewish calendar] all the people followed him to greet him. But when they saw Shemaya and Abtalion [scholars descended from converts] they forsook him and went after Shamaya and Abtalion. He [the high priest] said to them, "May the descendants of the heathen come in peace!"*
>
> *They [Shemaya and Abtalion] answered him [the high priest], "May the descendants of the heathen, who do the work of Aaron, arrive in peace, but the descendant of Aaron, who does not do the work of Aaron, he shall not come in peace."*[47]

One of the standard canards of anti-Semites today is that the Jews are racist. This spurious claim reached the height of infamy, when in November of 1975 the United Nations General Assembly passed Resolution 3379 declaring that Zionism is racism. Nothing could be further from the truth. Jews are not a race but rather comprise a nationality of people that began with a family, developed into a tribe, and coalesced into a nation that included the greater family of tribes and all "adopted" members. Moses, the greatest of prophets and most perfected of human beings, marries a convert, Jethro's daughter Tzipporah. Ruth, grandmother of King David, paradigm King of Israel, is also a convert.

What becomes of Jethro? Though not much is made apparent, there is some knowledge of his descendants. In the book of Judges we find, "The children of Kenite, Moses' father-in-law, ascended from the city of Date Palms with the children of Judah to he wilderness of Judah that is south of Arad; they went and settled with the people" (1:16). The great medieval commentator, Rabbi Shlomo Yitzhaki (more famously known by his acronym *Rashi)* explains that the city of Date Palms is none other than Jericho, the first major city miraculously conquered by Joshua upon Israel's entry into the Land. At the time, as today, Jericho was a verdant desert oasis with fine farmland. Joshua set aside that specific valuable tract of land to be given to the family upon whose land the Holy Temple would be built, as a means of compensation for surrendering their inheritance. This choicest of property was given to no other than Kenite, (another name for Jethro) Moses' father-in-law. Apparently Moses' offer to join and share in the blessings of the Children of Israel, was accepted.

Another fascinating epilogue to the episode of Jethro is found the book of Judges, when Deborah the prophetess summons Barak to lead the battle against Jabin, King of Canaan, and his renowned chief-of-staff, Sisera, oppressors of the Jewish people. Meanwhile we find mention of Jethro's (Hobab) descendants as we are told that, "Heber the Kenite had become separated from the Kenites, from the children of Hobab, father-in-law of Moses, and pitched his tents as far as the Plain of Zaanannim, which is near Kadesh" (4:11). Later, Hobab's descendants re-appear as we read the story of Yael, wife of Heber the Kenite, who manages to lure Sisera into her tent, and kill the elusive enemy by driving a tent peg through his temple (4:17-22).

That there was peace between the house of Heber the Kenite, (Jethro's family) and Jabin the Canaanite king of Hazor suggests that Jethro, or at least part of the family, did not convert and become part of the Jewish people. Perhaps a portion of the family did convert, and a part of the family remained righteous gentiles who recognized Jewish sovereignty in the land of Israel. Yael, of the Kenite clan, becomes the heroine in the mighty victory over Sisera and Jabin, vanquishing the oppressors of Israel, and the story of Jethro and his family remains a Biblical paradigm for the family of righteous Noahides, and a family of converts.

A Vision of Peace: The End of Days

Through the stirring orations of the prophets of the Hebrew Bible, we have a rich description of what are called the "end of days" in the Jewish tradition. In moving prose the prophet Isaiah describes this idyllic period, which has been etched into the cultural lexicon as the ultimate vision of peace:

> *It will happen in the end of days. The mountain of the Temple of God will be firmly established as the head of the mountains, and it will be exalted above the hills, and all the nations will stream to it. Many peoples will go and say, "Come, let us go up to the Mountain of God, to the Temple of the God of Jacob, and He will teach us of His ways and we will walk in His path." For from Zion will the Torah (Law) come forth, and the word of God from Jerusalem. He will judge among the nations, and will settle the arguments of many peoples. They shall beat their swords into plowshares and their spears into pruning hooks; nation will not lift sword against nations and they will no longer study warfare.*
>
> [Isaiah 2:24]

In his magnum opus *Mishneh Torah,* Maimonides describes what has become the normative Jewish view on the "end of days," or Messianic era. He bases his opinion on the declaration of the third century Talmudic sage Samuel that "the Messianic era differs from the present in nothing except that Israel will throw off the yoke of the nations and retain its political independence (Berachot 34b)." The world will continue its normal course; there will be wealthy and poor, and the laws of nature will function as always, except for the fact that Israel and the Jews will live in peace in Israel, with a Third and final rebuilt Temple. Lastly, the world will be filled with the pursuit of the knowledge of God and Torah (the Bible and Law).

The Jewish Messiah will be mortal, a descendant of King David, whose mission will be to rebuild the Sanctuary on the Temple Mount in Jerusalem and gather the dispersed people of Israel into a secure and sovereign Israel, replete with a Temple restored as the hub of a reawakened judicial, social, and spiritual world center.

Throughout millennia, from the time of the destruction of the Second Temple by the Romans in 70 C.E., throughout the centuries of dispersal, persecution, and oppression, Jews have longed for the restoration of their biblical homeland. Through crusades, pogroms, expulsions, blood libels, inquisitions, and the Holocaust, Jews have yearned and prayed for solace, acceptance and tranquility. In his Laws of Repentance, Maimonides beautifully formulates these centuries old yearnings:

> *Hence, all Israelites, their Prophets and Sages, prayed for the advent of Messianic times, that they might have relief from the wicked tyranny that does not permit them to properly occupy themselves with the study of Torah and the observance of the commandments; that they might have ease, devote themselves to getting wisdom, and thus attain a life in the world to come. Because the King who will arise will be from the seed of David and will have more wisdom than King Solomon and will be a great Prophet, approaching Moses our teacher, he will teach the whole of the Jewish people and instruct them in the ways of God; and all nations will come and hear him, as it is said "at the end of days it shall come to pass that the mount of the Lord's house shall be established as the top of the mountains" (Micah 4:1). The ultimate and perfect reward, the final bliss which will suffer neither interruption nor diminution is the life in the World-to-Come. The Messianic era, on the other hand, will be realized in this world, which will continue in its normal course except that independent sovereignty will be restored to Israel.*[49]

King David, second King of Israel, purchased the plot of land that was to become the site of the Temple Mount in Jerusalem from the Jebusites, with eyes set on building the First Temple. From the initial conquest of the land of Israel by Joshua, and throughout the period of the Judges, the Holy Ark, and the Tablets of Testimony found within, were contained in a portable sanctuary, or *Mishkan*. Its very purpose was to be mobile and temporary. Ultimately, it was clear that the *Mishkan* needed to be replaced by a permanent structure described literally dozens of times in the Bible as "the site that God your Lord shall choose [....] as a place dedicated to His name" (Deuteronomy 11:12). The Bible describes the vision and purpose of the Temple:

> *"These are the rules and laws that you must carefully keep in the land that God, Lord of your fathers, is giving you so that you will be able to occupy it as long as you live on earth. Do away with all the places where the [pagan] nations whom you are driving out worship their gods, [whether they are] on the high mountains, on the hills, or under any luxuriant tree. You must tear down their altars, break up their sacred pillars, burn their Asherah [pagan deity] trees, and chop down the statues of their gods, obliterate their names from that place. You may not worship God your Lord in such a manner. This you may do only at the site that God your Lord shall choose from among all your tribes, as a place established in His name. It is there that you shall go to seek his presence. That shall be the place to which you must bring your burnt offerings and eaten sacrifices, your tithes, and your hand delivered elevated gifts, your general and specific pledges, and the first born of your cattle and flocks. You and your families shall eat there before God your Lord and you shall rejoice in all your endeavors, through which God your Lord shall bless you. You will then not be able to do everything that we are now doing [where each] person does what is right in his eyes. Now you have not yet come to the resting place and hereditary land that God your Lord is giving you. But you shall soon cross the Jordan and live in the land that God your Lord is allotting you. When he has granted*

> *you safety from all your enemies around you, and you live in security, there will be a site that God will choose as the place dedicated to His name."*
>
> [Deuteronomy 12:1-14]

In an important work entitled *The Temple: Its Symbolism and Meaning Then and Now,* Joshua Berman explains the significance of the Temple not only as a spiritual center, but also as the focal point of the judicial, social, cultural, and political activity of the nation of Israel.[40] Notably, the Pentateuch always refers to the site of the Temple as "the site that God shall choose," for only when, as recounted above, the nation shall come "to the resting place and hereditary land" and shall have "safety from all your enemies" that the proper influence of the Temple could be felt. Until the children of Israel could settle the entire country and establish a viable and lasting sovereign government, capable of transferring authority to the next generation, it was premature to establish a capitol with a Temple, and all that it implies. This is because the Temple was not an exclusively Jewish institution, but rather a universal one, for all of mankind to enjoy and receive benefit.

The process of settling the land and establishing a sovereign government therein was not a simple task. Joshua, disciple and successor to Moses, began the conquest of the land of Israel in approximately 1100 BCE, after which political and spiritual authority after him was transferred to the Judges. These Judges ruled intermittently over the people of Israel for three to four hundred years in an era of "ups and downs," characterized by periods whereby the Israelites were subject to persecution by the local pagan city-states. It was not until the time of King David that the entire land was completely conquered and settled and the twelve tribes coalesced into the nation of Israel. It was only then that David was able to establish a national capitol. At the instruction of the prophet Nathan, the site of Jerusalem is divinely revealed (Samuel II 7:1-17).

David then proceeds to purchase the plot of land in Jerusalem upon which the Temple would ultimately be built. However, it was not fated for King David to build the Temple. As a king whose reign was characterized by warfare, David hands were too bloody to build a Temple that was to be an international symbol of peace. Instead, David's son, Solomon, an independent and secure ruler who showed unparalleled wisdom and enjoyed wholehearted acceptance from the nation, was destined for the task. The people respected his judgment and the nation enjoyed prosperity, peace, and tranquility, as had never before, or since been duplicated. The world's leaders recognized Israel and came to pay respects to King Solomon.

With this, the Patriarchs' dreams were now capable of being fulfilled. No matter how successful or charismatic the Patriarchs were, it was only in the context of a nation that their dream of building a society that would serve an example for the family of nations was to be realized. Only as a sovereign territory with the capability to sanctify the Lord in all aspects of temporal life, could Israel appropriately proclaim God's name. After centuries of development, the Jewish people had matured into a nation that was ready and capable of heralding this revolution of bringing God's message to the remainder of the family of nations

No longer would the Holy Ark be relegated to a temporary abode. It was now time to bring the message of the Ark – the Revelation of Sinai – to the rest of the world. As a unified family, Israel could powerfully convey the universal messages given to them, With a secure, prosperous, functioning government the ideal society envisioned in the Bible was capable of reaching fruition. Now the nations of the world could listen and emulate.

King Solomon's reign is described in the Book of Kings. Upon assuming the throne as a young man, Solomon prays for wisdom to guide the people justly. As a reward for his noble request, God grants him wisdom and much more. He presides over an elaborate government and his rule ushers in national joy and prosperity.

> *For he ruled over the entire area beyond the [Euphrates] River, from Tipsah to Gaza over all the kings of the area beyond the [Euphrates] River; and he was at peace [with the lands] on all sides, roundabout. Judah and Israel dwelt in security, each man under his*

> *grapevine and his fig tree, from Dan to Beer-Sheba, all the days of Solomon. God gave wisdom and considerable understanding to Solomon, and breadth of heart as [immense as] the sand which is upon the seashore [...] They came from all the nations to hear the wisdom of Solomon, [emissaries] from all the kings of the land who had heard of his wisdom.*
>
> [Kings I 5:4-5,14]

Solomon enlists the surrounding nations to aid in the construction of the Holy Temple, signing a covenant with the King of Tyre and enlisting the help of the Gebalites (Lebanese people skilled in masonry) to carve and prepare the wood and stones to build the Temple (Kings 5:21,32). We see that Hiram, and other righteous gentiles played a role in assisting Solomon to construct the Temple.

King Solomon makes two significant changes in the items included in the Temple in contrast to the Tabernacle, marking the more universalistic purpose of the Temple: In the Tabernacle, the *cherubim* (angelic winged figurines) graced the cover atop the Holy Ark. In the Temple however, the *cherubim* appear to be on the floor of the Holy of Holies (innermost sanctum of the Temple), their wings protectively embracing the entire ark" (Berman,79).

The symbolism is profound. God's word, initially proclaimed to the entire congregation of Israel at Sinai, continued to be heard by Moses throughout the desert wanderings. The stone Tablets of Testimony continued to serve as the focal point for the ongoing prophetic voice of God to Moses the prophet, and to all subsequent prophets who arose after Moses. Now, with the construction of the Temple, the voice of God — the prophetic encounter — was permanently centered in the Holy of Holies, in the Temple, in Jerusalem, capital of Israel, for the Jew and the entire world to hear.

In another significant change from the Tabernacle, Solomon replicates the *menorah*, the magnificent seven lamped candelabra, intricately, but rather than building one, Solomon builds ten. The seventy lights that emanated from the Temple would now spread to illuminate and enlighten the seventy nations that encompass the entire family of man.

After seven years of building, Solomon lifts his hands in prayer at the solemn inaugural ceremony upon the Temple's completion. He expresses gratitude to the God who had given him kingship and enabled him to build a habitation for the Divine presence, and beseeches God to answer the prayers emanating from within the Temple (Kings I 8:22-31). Solomon clearly does not designate the Temple as a house of prayer solely for Jews, but implores God to listen to the prayers of the gentiles who call out to Him from within its walls:

> *"Also a gentile who is not of your people Israel, but will come from a distant land, for your names sake (for they will hear of your great Name and your strong hand and outstretched arm) and will come and pray toward this Temple, may you hear from Heaven, the foundation of your abode, and act according to all that the gentile calls out to you, so that all the peoples of the world may know your name, to fear you as [does] your people Israel, and to know that your name is proclaimed upon this Temple that I have built."*
>
> [Kings I 8:41-44]

Nowhere is the universal aspect of the Jewish king's message so blatant. Solomon beseeches God to hear and grant the prayers of the gentile who recognizes Him— the Noahide. Solomon concludes his public prayer,

> *"Blessed is God Who has granted rest to His people Israel, according to all that He has spoken. Not one word has gone unfulfilled from the entire gracious promise that He pronounced through the hand of His servant Moses. May God, our Lord be with us as He was with our forefathers, may He not forsake us nor cast us off, to turn our hearts to Him, to walk in all His ways and to observe His commandments, decrees and statutes that He commanded our forefathers."*
>
> [Kings I 8:55-59]

The Divine promise to Abraham reached its fulfillment during Solomon's reign. Potentates and emissaries from all lands came to pay respect to Solomon and the Temple in Jerusalem, one of whom was the Queen of Sheba, who came from afar to test the limits of Solomon's wisdom and returned from the experience awe-stricken by the sagacity of Solomon's leadership (Chronicles II Chap 9:1-9).

Solomon's reign was a period where the ideal model society was established in the world, the zenith of the Abrahamic vision. It was a society internationally recognized as being one of "justice and righteousness." Unfortunately, it was too much, too fast. The success and splendor of Solomon's achievements did not last very long after his passing. The construction of the magnificent Temple was augmented with the building of elaborate palaces for himself and his many wives — particularly the daughter of Pharaoh of Egypt. For Solomon, serving as a "light unto the nations" meant being a temporal as well as a spiritual leader. As a result Solomon enacted heavy taxes to finance the major construction projects throughout the country and to develop a widespread military presence, creating some resentment amongst the populace.

In ancient times, good politics meant cementing alliances with neighboring countries by marrying into the royal family. Solomon, no doubt, through his wisdom and personality, sought to convey and spread the message of ethical monotheism and proactive fellowship through these political marriages. However the scripture tells us that he may have overestimated his capabilities, with "seven hundred wives who were noblewomen and three hundred concubines." Unfortunately, we learn that "his wives swayed his heart" to the negative (Kings 1 1:3). For all his brilliance, wisdom, and effort, Solomon had attempted to accomplish too much, too soon. While outwardly embracing the strictures of conversion to Judaism, or at least the adoption of the Noahide principles, it is apparent that they were not entirely sincere. Achieving a universal and lasting awareness of the importance of ethical monotheism and proactive fellowship is a slow, painstaking process — one in which we are all still engaged.

The Hebrew Bible does not spare harsh words even of its heroes, when deemed appropriate. That Solomon, in his old age, tolerated foreign idol worship amongst his many wives is presented through a stinging criticism of him: "So it was that when Solomon grew old his wives swayed his heart after the gods of others, and his heart was not as complete with the Lord God as [had been] the heart of his father David" (Kings II 11:4).

Solomon had not attained the wholehearted devotion of his father David and as a consequence his kingdom could not remain whole. After his father's passing, Rehavam, Solomon's son, assumes the throne. By initiating unpopular and excessive taxation Rehavam alienates the nation, and as a result his kingdom is split; ten of the tribes secede and form the Kingdom of Israel. The tribes of Judah and Benjamin, together with the priestly tribe of Levi, remain loyal to Rehavam in the smaller Kingdom of Judah.

In the book of Genesis, Judah and Joseph were the heroes who had brought the family together. Each had surrendered his own glory and preeminence for the good of the family. Judah had offered himself as a slave to save Benjamin from servitude; thereby achieving expiation for the kidnapping and sale of Joseph. Joseph, by engineering the scenario that gave the brothers the ability to make amends for their sin against him, relinquished the opportunity to exclude his ten brothers from inheriting their father's special legacy. The nation which had once begun the slow process of educating the whole of humanity now suffered a major setback.

For a period of approximately 200 years, from 930-732 B.C.E., the nation of Israel is divided into two kingdoms. In the year 732 B.C.E. the Northern Kingdom of Israel is conquered by the Assyrian empire and the ten tribes are sent into exile, dispersion, and eventual assimilation. They seem to be lost to the Jewish people. The Talmud debates whether any remnant of the ten tribes survived. The kingdom of Judah survived, and it is from there that the term "Jewish," meaning "from the children of Judah," is derived. In the year 586 B.C.E. the Holy Temple built by Solomon is destroyed by the Babylonians. The survivors of this bloody conquest are sent into exile to Babylonia, as the Kingdom of Judah comes to an end.

Not long after the Babylonian conquest of Jerusalem, the Persian Empire rises in prominence and the prophecies of Jeremiah and Ezekiel of a seventy year exile are fulfilled. Cyrus, king of Persia, issues a decree looking favorably upon the Jews' return to their homeland from Babylonia to rebuild their Temple. The Temple is rebuilt in the year 516 B.C.E. by "command of the God of Israel and by order of Cyrus and Darius and Artaxerxes, king of Persia" (Ezra 6:14). The Second Temple is also built with the help of righteous gentiles. Cyrus recognizes and attributes his success to the God of Heaven, who has charged him to build him a house in Jerusalem[53]:

> *Thus said King Cyrus of Persia, "The Lord God of Heaven has given me all the kingdoms of the earth and has charged me with building Him a house in Jerusalem, which is in Judah. Anyone of you, all His people – may his God be with him – and let him go up to Jerusalem that is in Judah and build the House of the Lord God of Israel, the God that is in Jerusalem, and all who stay behind, wherever he may be living, let the people of his place assist him with silver, gold, goods, and livestock, besides the freewill offering to the house of God that is in Jerusalem."*
>
> [Ezra 1:2-4]

The Second Temple is constructed. However this structure lacks the majesty of the First Temple. The prophet Haggai bemoans this reality:

> *Who is there left among you who saw this House in its former splendor? How does it look to you now? It must seem like nothing to you! But be strong oh Zerubavel, says the Lord, be strong! Oh high priest Joshua son of Yehozadak, be strong all you people of the land, says the Lord – and act! For I am with you, says the Lord of Hosts. So I promised you when you came out of Egypt, and My spirit is still in your midst, fear not!*
>
> [Haggai 2:3-5]

Unfortunately, only a small number of Jews, amounting to about 42,000, answered the call to return to Israel from Babylonia (Ezra 2:64). The overwhelming majority of Jews exiled to Babylonia were apparently content in their new lives, lacking the fortitude to return. Again the consequences of dissension within the community of Israel adversely affected their ability to proactively inspire the remainder of humanity. With the notable exception of the Hasmonean rebellion and the subsequent period of independence, most of the period of the Second Commonwealth saw national sovereignty lacking. Without national sovereignty, how could the Jewish nation develop a society that would be a model nation?

The Second Temple stood for 420 years, mostly during semi-autonomous periods under Persian, Greek, and Roman rule. For a short period, the Hasmonean kings from the tribe of Levi succeeded in achieving independence for the Jewish state. However, the final days of the Second Temple were characterized by bitter infighting among the different sects of Jews, some of whom sought independence from Rome. A revolution against Rome ensued, with tragic consequences for the entire Jewish people, as the revolution was brutally suppressed and the Temple was destroyed. Jews became dispersed throughout the Roman Empire and two millennia of exile followed.

The Talmud describes the internecine disputes amongst the Jewish factions as the cause of the final destruction. In a pithy example of the time, the Talmud describes a lavish feast given by a wealthy Jerusalemite. This citizen of Jerusalem had a friend named "Kamza" and an enemy named "Bar-Kamza." The nameless citizen hosts a lavish party and instructs his servant to invite "Kamza" to the banquet, but the servant mistakenly brings "Bar Kamza" to the affair. At seeing his enemy at the affair, the host accosts his guest, saying, "What are you doing here? Get out!" Embarrassed, Bar Kamza, the uninvited guest, replies to the host, "Since I am here, let me stay and I will pay you for whatever I eat and drink." The host is insistent. Bar Kamza then implores the host, "If you do not embarrass me publicly, I will pay for half the cost of the affair." Bar Kamza then offers to pay the cost of the entire banquet, if only he is not humiliated into leaving. The host subsequently takes Bar Kamza by the hand and ejects him from the party. The prominent Rabbis, also guests at the party, did nothing to prevent the scene of his humiliation and this spurs Bar Kamza to assume that their silence reflected their complicity. Incensed and vengeful, Bar Kamza informs the Roman government that the Jews are plotting a revolution against the Roman emperor.[54]

Ultimately, Jerusalem is besieged and the population is starved. Various sects of Jews war against each other, thereby preventing a unified response aimed at reconciliation or credible military action against Rome. Jerusalem is sacked and the Temple is destroyed in the year 70 C.E. Again the tragic results of dissension within the family bode poorly for the Jewish people and their mission to become a "light unto the nations."

Looking forward however, the Bible posits that the current state of affair need not be permanent. The prophet Haggai presents a vision of the third and final Temple, in all its glory, permanence ,and universality:

> *For thus said the Lord of Hosts: "In just a little while longer I will shake the heavens and the earth, the sea and the dry land. I will shake all the nations. And the precious things of all the nations shall come here, and I will fill this House with glory," said the Lord of Hosts. "Silver is Mine and gold is Mine" —, says the Lord of Hosts. "The glory of this latter House shall be greater than that of the former one," said the Lord of Hosts, "and in this place I will grant prosperity," declares the Lord of Hosts.*
>
> [Haggai 2:6-9]

The prophet Ezekiel as well, who prophesied during the Babylonian captivity, saw an ultimate reconciliation within the family; one that would have worldwide implications:

> *The word of God came to me saying, "Now you, Son of Man [Ezekiel], take for yourself one piece of wood and write upon it 'for Judah and for the Children of Israel,*

his comrades,' and take a piece of wood and write upon it, 'For Joseph, the wood of Ephraim and all the House of Israel, his comrades.' Then bring them close to yourself, one to the other, like one piece of wood, and they will become united in your hand Now when the children of your people say to you, saying, 'Will you not tell us what these things are to you?' – say to them: 'Thus said the Lord God: Behold, I am taking the wood of Joseph which is in the hand of Ephraim, and the tribes of Israel, his comrades, and I am placing them and him together with the wood of Judah; and I will make them into one piece of wood, and they will become one in My hand....

Behold I am taking the Children of Israel from among the nations to which they have gone; I will gather them from all around and I will bring them to their soil. I will make them into one nation in the land, upon the mountains of Israel, and one king will be a king for them all. They will no longer be two nations and they will no longer be divided into two kingdoms, ever again. They will no longer be contaminated with their idols and with their abhorrent things and with all their sins. I will save them [take them] from all their dwelling places in which they had sinned, and I will purify them; they will be a nation to Me, and I will be a God to them. My servant David will be king over them, and there will be one shepherd for all of them; they will follow My ordinances and keep my decrees and fulfill them. They will dwell on the land that I gave to My servant Jacob, within which your fathers dwelled; they and their children and their children's children will dwell upon it forever. I will seal a covenant of peace with them, it will be an eternal covenant with them, and I will emplace them and increase them, and I will place My Sanctuary among them forever. My dwelling place will be among them, I will be a God to them and they will be a people to Me. Then the nations will know that I am God Who sanctifies Israel, when My sanctuary will be among them forever."

[Ezekiel 37:15-28]

Epilogue: The Current State of World Affairs

The 20th century was characterized as a conflict between socio-political systems: communism-fascism versus capitalism-democracy.

The close of the 20th century seemed to mark the demise of communism and signify the victory of capitalism. The Soviet Union imploded and its former bloc of nations scrambled to import the panacea of open markets and free enterprise. The world was captivated by what was apparently endless growth of personal consumption and material prosperity. However unbridled capitalism had its lurking dangers. The financial markets governing the capitalist system were quick to respond to an unprecedented increase in consumer demand and met this burgeoning demand with ever-increasing levels of debt. Nowhere was this increased borrowing more apparent than in the housing sector.

A man's most important and vital sense of security and well being may be attributed to owning one's own home – his own place of dwelling – to shelter himself and his immediate family. Along with food and clothing, this is the most basic human need. In the early 21st century, the financial markets were telling the consumer the equivalent of, "Go ahead, we will lend you $200,000 for the house that you paid $100,000 for. We will charge you interest for sure, but you can always sell your house for much more than you paid, and things are good – so no need to worry!" Homeowners were enraptured by the seemingly easy money and encouraged to borrow more and more. Financial companies kept on lending and lending because the financial instruments they invented promised quick, huge profits. This endless pursuit of expanded borrowing imploded in the financial breakdown of 2008. The immediate effect of the financial crisis is the insecurity and inability of so many millions of people to afford their own homes – from which comes their primary sense of security and well being.

The bottom line will bring what many believe to be a deep, extended depression, high unemployment, and a protracted reduction in the standard of living enjoyed by most people. It is only hoped that social dislocation and unrest will be mitigated by wise and prudent leadership.

Unbridled capitalism, fueled by simple greed, created a reality wherein the financial instruments so widely utilized in our modern economy were misused and misappropriated by those entrusted to guard it. In the quest for quick and large "paper profits" for the few, the economic wellbeing and security of our society has been undermined and badly damaged. In a prescient chapter of the prophet Ezekiel, this phenomenon is exposed and addressed.

The last eight chapters in the book of Ezekiel describe vividly the design and structure of the Third and final Temple in Jerusalem. With the reinstitution of the Temple service, there will also be a reallocation of the Land of Israel according to the Tribal units. Each of the twelve tribes will receive an equal portion from north to south. Further subdivisions between members of each tribe to family clan, to household, to individual family head ensure that each man has a portion of land and rights to his own home. Furthermore , as described in the Hebrew Bible, each has the right to his own entitlement – because the land belongs to God – and so He decrees. Amazingly, Ezekiel, in chapter 45, refers to the sovereign in Israel at this future time with the Hebrew term *nasi*, "president" – not "king" or "prince."

The president of Israel is admonished for gifting any other individual's land in Israel to his sons. If the president wishes to gift land – it must be from his own homestead. Property rights, the fundamental human need for a sense of security and well being, is recognized by the Bible and preserved by what we have noted earlier in our work as the Jubilee cycle. We also suggested that the 613 Biblical precepts may serve as an example for the remainder of the nations of the world. The single Noahide positive precept of a system of justice provides the framework for each sovereign country and society to enact those laws which it deems proper and benevolent to its members. This becomes an elective for each country as it advances and improves itself.

> *"You are to divide this land among yourselves for the tribes of Israel. And thus shall be what you allocate as a heritage for yourselves and for the strangers [converts] among you, who bear children in your midst. They shall be considered by you as citizens in the family of Israel with you, they are to be allotted an inheritance among the tribes of Israel."*
>
> [Ezekiel 47:21-2]

Ezekiel boldly asserts that in the end of Days, we will recognize and respect this basic human need.

We began this work with a rhetorical question posed by the prophet Malachi: Why the dissension amongst nations, within nations? How can we be so blind to the Godliness which ties us together? Though the exquisite prophetic dialogue between God and the children of Israel was silenced, it is waiting to be reawakened during the Messianic era. Malachi implores us to re-examine the common threads of humanity among us, if we are going to attempt to repair the brokenness of the world. Only then will the family of nations be whole once again.

Endnotes

[1] *Zohar Yitro* 87A. See also commentary of Nachmanides to *Book of Genesis*, chapter 1.

[2] *Deuteronomy* 31:9 in *The Living Torah*, translated by Rabbi Aryeh Kaplan (Moznaim Publishing 1981)

[3] *Babylonia Talmud (BT) Menahot* 29b, translated by Eli Cashdan (Traditional Press 1980)

[4] Dr. Gerald L Schroeder, *Genesis and the Big Bang, the Discovery of Harmony Between Modern Science and the Bible* (Bantam Books 1990) p. 49-50

[5] Nathan Aviezer, *In the Beginning, Biblical Creation and Science* (New Jersey: Ktav Publishing 1990) p. 66-68

[6] Aviezer p. 70

[7] Aviezer p. 72

[8] Commentary of Rabbi David Qimchi to *Genesis* 9:13

[9] *BT Sanhedrin* 70A. See also *Midrash Tanhuma Noah* 15

[10] Commentary of Hizkuni to *Genesis* 10:32

[11] *Bereshit Rabbah* 38:10

[12] *BT Sanhedrin* 56-58

[13] John Hick, *The Existence of God* (Routledge Kegan & Paul) p. 23

[14] *ibid.* p. 71

[15] *ibid.* p. 23

[16] John Hick, editor, *Classical and Contemporary Readings in the Philosophy of Religion* (New Jersey: Prentice Hall 1970)

[17] Steven Cahn, *Philosophy of Religion: The Irrelevance to Religion of Philosophic Proofs for the Existence of God* (New York: Harper & Row 1970) p. 273

[18] *BT Sanhedrin* 56a

[19] *BT Sanhedrin* 59b

[20] Aaron Lichtenstein, *The Seven Laws of Noah* (New York: The Rabbi Jacob Joseph School Press 1981) p. 31-35

[21] *BT Sanhedrin* 109a

[22] Menahem Leibtag, *Commentary on Parshat Toldot* (Tanach Study Center, Alon Shvut Israel)

[23] R. Israel Chait, *Jewish Times* (12/7/07 weekly edition)

[24] Commentary of Rashi to *Genesis* 49:28

[25] R. Bernie Fox, "Commentary on Parshat Vayehi" *Jewish Times* (12/21/07)

[26] William James, *The Varieties of Religious Experience* (New York: Simon & Schuster 1997) p. 42

[27] *ibid.* p. 59

[28] *ibid.* p. 72

[29] *ibid.* p. 74

[30] *ibid.* p. 86

[31] *ibid.* p. 114-129

[32] *ibid.* p. 220, quoting Dr. W. R. Inge (London 1899) in his *Lectures on Christian Mysticism*

[33] *ibid.* p. 301

[34] *ibid.* p. 268

[35] Jacob S. Minkin, *The Teachings of Maimonides* (New Jersey: Jason Aronson Inc 1987) p. 293

[36] Moses Maimonides, *The Guide of the Perplexed*, translated by Shlomo Pines (Chicago: Chicago University Press 1967) Book II Chap. 32 p. 360

[37] *ibid.* Book II Ch 35 p. 367

[38] *Minkin*, p. 305

[39] Jose Faur, *The Horizontal Society: Understanding the Covenant and Alphabetic Judaism* (Brighton, Mass.: Academic Studies Press 2008) p. 223

[40] Samuel P Huntington, *The Clash of Civilizations and the Remaking of World Order* (New York: Simon & Schuster 2003) p. 45-48

[41] *ibid.* p. 81-95

[42] Eliyahu Benamozegh, *Jewish & Christian Ethics, translated from the French* (San Francisco: Emanual Blochman Publishing 1873) p. 21

[43] *ibid.* p. 36

[44] "Hagee, Falwell Deny Endorsing Dual Covenant Theology" *Jerusalem Post* (March 2006)

[45] Joel Richardson, *Will Islam Be Our Future? A Study of Biblical & Islamic Eschatology*, chapter 15

[46] *BT Sanhedrin* 56a

[47] *BT Yoma* 71b

[48] *BT Berachot* 34b

[49] Moses Maimonides, *Mishneh Torah: Laws of Kings* chapters 9-10

[50] Minkin, p. 399, quoting *Mishneh Torah*

[51] *Samuel II* 24:24

[52] *BT Sanhedrin* 110B

[53] Joshua Berman, *The Temple: Its Symbol and Meaning Then and Now* (New Jersey: Jason Aronson Inc 1995) p. 163

[54] *BT Gittin* 55

About the Author

Joseph Haddad is an American living in Israel for the past 15 years. While professionally engaged in international trade the author has also pursued a lifelong passion for Bible and spiritual studies.

Born in New York City, the author was a member of the first graduating class of Touro College in 1975. He later pursued graduate studies at the Bernard Baruch Graduate School of Business.

In 1993 the author together with his wife Sharon and 6 children made *aliya* to Israel. They reside in Rananna.

Weekly classes in Bible studies are conducted in the author's home on the Sabbath.